I0100928

HUMAN EXISTENCE

HUMAN EXISTENCE
What Makes Life Worth Living

C. DAVID MORTENSEN

IPBOOKS.net

International Psychoanalytic Books (IPBooks)
New York • http://www.IPBooks.net

HUMAN EXISTENCE: What Makes Life Worth Living

Published by IPBooks, Queens, NY
Online at: www.IPBooks.net

Copyright © 2020 C. David Mortensen

All rights reserved. This book may not be reproduced, transmitted, or stored, in whole or in part by any means, including graphic, electronic, or mechanical without the express permission of the author and/or publisher, except in the case of brief quotations embodied in critical articles and reviews.

ISBN: 978-1-949093-76-6

CONTENTS

1

The Larger Scheme of Things

L ife on earth is made possible by the way the universe works. In an infinite universe, anything is possible but a tiny speck of intelligent civilization arises as rare, singular and unique. Stars, planets, and galaxies are formed out of collapsing clouds of gas, dusk, gravitation, and magnetic force fields. Cosmic dusk contains water, in the form of ice, plus hydrogen, helium, oxygen, carbon, iron, nitrogen. Ice clusters change in outer space, from vaper into solids, building up into sticks of larger grains of colliding material. Friction, heat, light, and electric forces hold sticky grains together in colliding particles, complex enough to tug on each other by the force of gravity. Planet formation evolves into states of massive complexity. Clusters of molecules emerge from carbon, hydrogen, oxygen, and nitrogen, four common elements in the universe and the inanimate basis for the chemistry of life. Living organisms utilize only those chemical compounds that are available to them.

Organic chemistry is synonymous with carbon chemistry. The most widely known life molecule is DNA, a molecule in the cells of all thriving organisms, including ourselves, an imprint of living code. Genetic programs contain tacit instructions that guide fertilized cells to operate in a specific way. Another molecule, RNA, functions the same as DNA, with oxygen atoms removed. The code of life transfers implicit messages, basic components of DNA, into material significance. Proteins function as molecules of living substances, as found in all forms of life on Earth.

Astronomers have made astonishing progress in mapping shifting contours of an expansive universe. Dim origins can be traced back through dense clouds and dusk though 13.7 billion years of colliding particles, heat, light, and dark expanse. Several billion years of 'habitable' planets in the Galaxy have exceeded all the people living on planet earth. However, whatever qualifies as 'habitable' does not assure 'inhabited' conditions. The larger scheme of things does not easily reveal dark secrets or give way to repeated performances. Mortal existence, therefore, is a spectacular, singular achievement. The combination of living organisms, inanimate objects, and non-living processes contributes to the inter-relatedness of life on Earth. It has taken adaptive intelligence over the course of some four billion years to transform a rocky planet into a technological civilization. We are here because of cosmic catastrophes so improbable, incalculable, as to make our planet unique and a urgent need to face our collective destiny alone. Such an ecological miracle may be construed as worthy of a revered stance of wonder and awe.

Material implications follow. Massive combinations of matter and energy show that design does not 'start' at a fixed point of origin. Physical force is magnified by interactions of simple molecules that congeal into complex aggregates of substantive material. Hence, living and nonliving components intersect through invisible feedback mechanisms to stabilize and maintain suitable conditions for living organisms to persist and thrive. No direct mode of consciousness is involved. Human beings are not aware of varied, intricate, and scaled feedback processes which regulate metabolism, heart rate, and temperature to keep regulatory functions more or less constant. The vitality of living organisms is due to mechanical, automatic, and unintentional aspects of non-living properties. The universe is not conscious of what makes it possible but still determines what human existence makes possible. Creation is not a product of intelligent design, or supreme designer, but rather due to organic entities of earthly habitation.

Matter and Energy

A material model is not the only one available. Idealism favors the path to perfection, infallibility, eternal mandates. Subjectivism invites seductive appeal to reductive formulas: meaning is perception, the sky is the limit, mind over matter, self-help (books), believing makes it so, fundamentalism (eternal security). Intractable dogma is not far behind: grim appeal to survival of the fittest, might makes right, sovereignty of rules, roles, and norms. Agentic models confuse matters of causation with correlation—whereby human behaviors get all the credit while forceful penetration of physical forces are ignored or left behind (as though setting, situation, context, and circumstance are merely dispatched as distant incidental properties). Simplified narratives may work out well to account for ordinary habits and routines. Mortality issues, however, are not easily swept away, regardless of false claims of social desirability that would leave physical laws behind.

The meaning of life unfolds in an open field of possibilities. Sustained inquiry enhances the search for alternatives. Life signals vitality. Animated movements register as strategic activity. Meaning produces signals, signs, and symbols of valuation, preference, and priority. Attributional features include a center, periphery, and horizon of definition, classification, and explanation. Sensations and perceptions blend into conceptions (interpretation).

All facts are value laden. Standards of inclusion (proximity) outweigh measures of exclusion (distance). The wider search for meaning leads from points of identity, direction, concern and care to the discovery of something that matters. A meaningful way of life is inscribed as the ultimate achievement (among) inspiring aspirations. Mortal existence is rare, precious, and unique—simply because no compelling alternatives are subject to reproduction or replication.

Universal meaning systems coalesce into finite spheres of sustained inquiry. Universality signifies collective systems of relevance, as exemplified in whole realms of matter, activity, or existence. Vitality requires direct access to scarce ecological resources. Some things apply to all of the people all of the time, even though some material conditions may not align in a uniform or equitable manner. Valuations are transitory. Nothing lasts forever. Change is constant. Life never lasts long enough to get everything done. Claims of human struggle are tentative, fragile, precarious. Finite features of life (foreground) unfold against an infinite (background) of ecological force and cosmic turmoil.

Vigor and Vitality

Human vitality is embedded in a wider array of prior conditions (assumptions), present disclosers (transactions), and future expectations (anticipations). Personal meaning systems are modified so we can live with ourselves. Concerted effort is required to align past, present, and future valuations into the larger flow of goal-directed aims. Self-awareness does not rise above (or transcend) the upper limits of organic striving. To pretend otherwise is to indulge in pure fiction. Conscious intentions do not secure desired outcomes. The law of unintended consequences is alive and well. Negotiated outcomes cannot be fully calculated in advance. Distinctions between explicit manifestations (transparency) and implicit disclosures (mystery) are subject to the press of vague and uncertain aspects of short-term results and long-term consequences.

One implication is clear. There is no master plan to guide our way through the maze of confounding difficulties that cloud our path. It is not possible to maintain full control over what happens to us. Human agents must struggle to survive in local confines of a habitable world that is given rather than chosen. In the end, the sheer force of physical laws will prevail over the impact of social rules.

On a larger scale, each moment of birth is subject to transitory conditions of living and dying across the life span. Every living agent is endowed (as producer and product) of evolutionary (intergenerational) modifications acquired from a (pre)existing world view (legacy, tradition). Genetic codes (imprints) filter (in and out) of embedded constructions of conflicted social interaction. So much of what transpires across the lifespan is not subject to the whims of volitional control or intentional choice. Even so-called 'conscious awareness' is fashioned out deeper, historic, evolved forces that elude our grasp.

The case for predestination: Fate is inevitable. Viable organisms are thrown into a preexisting world without any choice in what transpires before or after their rise and fall. No one chooses to be a source of life or death. Kinship ties are inherited. Attention is selective. So is literacy. Obligations and opportunities exist side by side. Experience accumulates in the manner of trial-and-error. Everyone is left to bear their own burdens. No one's lived experience can take the place of anyone else.

Therefore, presumptive claims of volition and 'free' choice are never "free" historic forces that linger in the background of diffuse cultural tensions. Habits and routines require (biased) access to scarce resources required to reproduce their uniformity. At all times and in all places, meaning systems are products of what makes their specific references credible. Therefore, internalized meanings are mostly responses, not main causes, of the sheer press of external events that penetrate into the interior depths of body boundaries. Biological forces are never brought under total societal control. *Collective values are mutual expressions of those who make our lives worth living and our expressions that make others worth living.* Human survival is a collective rather than an isolated achievement.

There is no such thing as a static or inert sense of universal inquiry. Temporal and spatial meanings of mortality evolve, rise, and fall within the wider province of infinite realms of possibility (context). Physical activities may rise (ascend), dissolve (descend), shift (change), regress (backward) or progress (forward across time and space. Three broad types of dynamic change are implicated. One, lateral movements resonate close by (proximity) or far away (distance). Two, hierarchical movements shift upward (credit) or downward (discredit). Three, salient shifts alternate between salient (relevant) and incidental (irrelevant) markers. By pragmatic standards, the privileged meanings of a life well lived gain traction from ascendant, progressive, and credible valuations. Conversely, loss of meaning implies distance, regression, and discredit of prevailing or privileged valuations.

The larger scheme of things also comes into play. Finite adjustments in social influence (transitory effects) may blend into infinite identities of a prevailing world view (encompassing results). Human meaning systems are necessarily embedded in larger, inclusive force fields: integration or disintegration, location or dislocation, accessible or inaccessible territory, along with habitable or inhabitable boundaries. Life on planet earth is precarious because physical laws regulate the universe (by force), whereas social rules (by persuasion) are left to dissolve into human encounters that assume symbolic form.

Force and Influence

The collective impact of infinite force fields and finite societal influence are not mutually exclusive. Physical forces are causal mechanism that penetrate from outside to inside of body boundaries (cold, storms, fires). Social influences are reactive responses that gravitate from inside to outside of human activity (clothes, shelter, sprinklers). In transactional terms, common sense can work two ways at once, either to minimize harmful effects of natural toxicity (dirty energy) or to use social influence as a forceful means of intervention (clean energy) In effect, societal collaborations can mitigate the severity of physical force (guns, weapons), or subdue material laws through progressive intervention (disarmaments, peace treaties).

Much depends on whether there is sufficient provision for human beings to live in harmony with nature. When the balance between nature and nurture is upset (asymmetry), prior meanings may be rendered meaningless, misguided, or obsolete. A life worth living implicates global preservation of material resources, along with life affirming values, as a resolute means to sustain the outer limits of human longevity. What is at stake is an abiding and resilient sense of honor, dignity, and due regard for the planet along with the preservation of all existing life forms. We are *human* by virtue of biological definition. We acquire *humane* status by way of engaging in exemplary forms of cultural conduct, so no one or nothing of value is left out of the sweeping equation. Individual, social, and collective worth is ultimately worth preserving, despite all the malignant forces that are set against it.

The visible universe, technically speaking, was not created but rather constructed out of the chaotic force of colliding particles. Ancient models of creation ignore a primordial fact: the origins of the visible universe were not the (personal) products of intelligent design, but rather made manifest by the sheer might of colliding (impersonal) force fields. Stars, comets, and planets are neither intelligent nor designed. It is a misleading to assign intentions, motives, or plans to inanimate objects. Life did not emerge from divine inspiration or supernatural purpose. Rather the big bang lead to billions of years of destructive expansivity. It is hard to imagine the reproduction of viable life forms that are not derived from an original mass of colliding energy. Stars, planets, and solar systems are not designed to 'live' or 'die' but rather rise and fall across staggering displacements of time and space.

By implication, finite meanings and infinite possibilities are closely fused together. The universe (larger scheme of things) cannot be displaced or dispatched into some dark corner of ancient light. Everything that transpires on planet earth is made possible by an infinitely expansive universe. Human activities emerge from matter that produces energy which in turn makes possible co-evolution of language, technology, and symbolic artifacts. The activation of sensory organs is necessary to produce basic rudiments of active meaning systems, based on an acquired means of capacity, ability, and use. Similar operations hold for what is seen, heard, spoken, touched, or moved. Words and gestures work the same way. Literate articulations can only be sustained by mechanisms of vigor and vitality. Human beings do not 'create' identity. Living organisms are constructed out of the physical objects that light up the night sky or spread sunshine during the day. The larger scheme of things is what makes meaning possible, for gain of for loss.

The meaning of meaning is not easily obtained. It takes time, space, and labor-intensive effort to assign life affirming values to the flux and flow of arbitrary or fabricated events. If everything is meaningful, then nothing is meaningless. If every sensation, perception, and conception is equally weighed, it would be virtually impossible to assign priorities, privileges, and preferences to chaotic or random events. There must, therefore, be minimal provision for attention, inspection, and concentration on goal-directed aims.

There is only so much time to focus on what matters more or less and only so much space to move around alternative vantage points. The consumption of temporal and spatial expenditure of matter and energy are baselines measures of what qualifies as worthy or unworthy of creative investments. Some people, places, and things are not worth the effort required to notice, much less attend to detailed inspection. Some efforts are more trouble than they are worth. It is quite impossible to be everything to everyone all the time. There is only enough energy and matter to go around. Preliminary consideration is based on standards of inclusion and exclusion of potential discoveries.

Success and Failure

Assigned meanings are fallible. It is always possible to be mistaken. Definitions of identification and misidentification are not always self-evident or easy to sort out. Sense-making efforts do not always make good sense. Distinctive human enterprises are at risk. Of central concern is the sheer complexity of forces and factors that make things turn out the way they do, for better or for worse. Success or failure registers on a dramatic scale, in the fulfillment of complex intentions, objectives, and goals in complex public settings. Ordinary interpretations remain, to some extent, a matter of hit or miss, trial-and-error. Other attributions may miss the target altogether. Misidentification stems from reading too much into little things (false positives) or leave too much out of little things (false negatives). The search for meaning requires a stance of resolute persistence, in spite of mistake, miscue, or miscalculation. In effect, making sense together requires hard work, regular practice, and tolerance of uncertainty, confusion, and ambiguity.

Meaning systems are subject to multiple tests of validity and reliability in an uncertain and precarious world. Virtually all supportive, caring, and constructive endeavors can be neutralized or undermined by the subversive impact of unknown, uncertain, or unpredictable factors that give rise to diverse states of prolong discomfort or unpredictable distress. In effect, personal appraisals provide multiple standards of critical assessment that make things better or keep them from getting worse. The effects of 'gain' or 'loss' may add valuation to meaning or take it away.

What it means to be a human being cannot be settled in the abstract or else simply resolved on narrow theoretical grounds. Over the lifespan, each person is endowed with the greater potential to be located where when something happens, to discover something that matters, and test the magnitude of desired effect against the cumulative margin of unwanted error. What is affordable is an unspecified measure of tentative, uncertain, and provisional opportunity to participate in the composite features and dense textures of everyday life. Productive achievements require intentional, purposeful, and strategic commitments to the fulfillment of complex tasks, projects, and routines in a material world that is brightly illuminated by intricate webs of elaborated significance.

Human encounters are labor-intensive. Making sense of the complex conduct of other people requires a great deal of time, energy, and effort. Collective effort to make sense of things takes place at two levels: strategic (intentional, conscious, purposeful) and automatic (unintended, unconscious, mechanistic) devices. This dual process activates modes of meaning and significance, alongside explicit (observable) and implicit (inferential) references.

The distinction between meaningful sense and meaningless nonsense matters greatly. Speaking subject generate references of significance, whether favorable or not, to absorb an array of particulars into an enduring sense of shared knowledge. For these reasons, the pursuit of a life worth living does not unfold on narrow individualistic grounds but rather on multiple, collective tests of what is deemed worthy of emulation. In other words, social interaction gives rise to the possibility, but not the necessity, of finding something of communicative value (relevance).

The capacity secure strong ties with other people ranks among the most frequent sources of privileged meaning in mortal existence. The search for a life well lived may be envisioned as a quest, a journey, and arduous process of constant probing, questioning, and testing generated by all the tensions, contradictions, triumphs, and tragedies of everyday life. The search for resolute or efficacious meaning qualifies, therefore, as a universal motive, as a means of belonging, as a pathway to worthwhile endeavor, and as a fundamental way to understand one's place in the world. Sophisticated reflection about one's encounter with predicaments, quandaries, and contradictions is a condition of the good life. Likewise, a personal sense of meaningful engagement is also a vital factor in preserving a coherent worldview and strong sense of well-being over the life span.

In effect, a life worth living implies an abiding commitment to achieve states of optimum fulfillment, revealed as an inclusive sense of significance, worth, and validation. In contrast, concern about the inability to find meaning in life may mask a broader clinical syndrome (depression, compulsion, addiction, or stress disorder) or aggravated problems in living with obstacles, barriers, false starts, and resistance to worthwhile endeavors. Excluded or rejected individuals may enter into a defensive state that avoids all meaningful thought, feeling, or awareness. Lethargy, listlessness, and slow reactions are not likely to be highly valued.

Summary

Mortal existence is embedded in the larger scheme of things. Genetic codes facilitate the proliferation of animated modes of human activity. Conscious awareness accounts for far less sensory activity than covert aspects of unconscious urges, needs, desires of goal-directed aims. Matter and energy determine the vigor and vitality of personal projects. The search for meaning culminates in the discovery of something that matters. The length, duration, and intensity of longevity expectations are largely predetermined, rather than merely freely chosen. Physical laws comingle with social influences as shared means to regulate creative inquiry. Meaning systems are resilient yet fragile. A life well lived resonates in close bonds with kindred spirits. There is no assurance that success will dispel failure.

2

Favorable Conditions

A life worth living occurs when striving subjects are able to preserve and protect privileged valuations in daily life. Physical settings vary in productive aims and tactical advantages. Here 'favorable' aligns with suitable applications. Matter and energy, vigor and vitality, foster personal goals and social aims. Favorable and unfavorable conditions blend together when stable locations shift into unstable tensions. Favorable conditions can easily dissolve into adverse events without appeal of constructive aims. Climate change: sunny days to stormy nights, forest growth to wild fires, calm seas to raging storms, safe traffic to road rage.

The desire to live well is reality tested when favorable options misalign with unfavorable constraints. Survival validates resolve to overcome obstacles. Options multiply with firm resolve to invest in worthy causes larger than ourselves. A life well lived produces robust meaning systems (justifications) that cannot be achieved any other way than by tolerance of struggle, strife, and strain. It is difficult, therefore, to envision the realization of optimal conditions in the absence of a disciplined way of life (higher calling). The ability to live fully, moment by moment, one day at a time, gives way to a greater latitude of discovery across the life course. Meaningful outcomes tend to expand outward, from personal competence, relational compatibility, community participation, to unflinching concern for the welfare of other people.

There are no magic formulas for living well or lasting a long time. Finite existence unfolds with mixed desires: gain blends with loss, positivity invites negativity, success risks failure. Some things make matters better; other things make them worse. Nothing gets everything figured out (once and for all). Uncertainty and ambiguity are intrinsic features of earthly bargains.

One mortal principle holds: there is one life to live. Each life span is inscribed as singular, unique, non-replicable. Once life is over, it is finally over. Nor longer is it possible to recover prior ability to see, hear, say, touch, move or notice what takes place in secular terms. No one can come back and start all over again. Reality is stark. Mortal existence matters when it is called in question, in jeopardy, or in short supply. When time rules out, so does space to move around.

World population, now almost eight billion strong, tests the resilience of the human spirit, despite whatever odds are set against it. Evolution is reassuring. The 'end' of one generation makes possible the 'start' of another generation. Human legacies shift the weight of valued meanings outward, away from narrow parameters, toward a wider array of life spans. Thereby, it is possible to live for the sake of those who arrive, before, during, or after our own finite existence. The value of each life acquires significance in light of what makes it possible and what it enables future generations to sustain. Each life, regardless of impact, adds to the ultimate value of historic and cultural legacies.

Since the dawn of civilization, more procreative failures, abortions, dead babies, and short life spans have exceeded the total number of persons who have ever survived to the outer limits of their projected life spans. Of all the persons who have ever existed on planet Earth, less than ten percent are still alive today. Every living person will perish in a century or less. Death may be the final arbitrator but it does not arrive at the 'end' but rather in the midst of all the life that surrounds it.

There is no way to insure finite existence beyond the outer limits of tolerance and forbearance. Requisite conditions—birth, living, dying, and death—are prescribed, as a legacy of what has transpired across generations. The past registers as memory, instruction, and guidance for current activities which in turn are projected, through expectation, into an uncertain future. Personal narratives are linked together, revealed in a script, envisioned as a journey, without provision for closure. Life integrates what death disintegrates. What makes life precious and resilient merits recognition as fragile and precarious.

Everyday life is subject to severe reality tests. Obstacles and opportunities are not freely chosen, but sustained under shifting levels of risk and hazard. Favorable features are neither self-evident nor transparent. Daily events unfold, without certainty or clarity, to guide progressive or regressive pathways into further inquiry. Mortal existence implicates two broad types of adaptive resilience. One, striving subjects must be able to adapt to change, whether from situational constraints or behavioral pressures. Two, environmental resources must be accessible to insure human accommodation. Four broad types of capacities, abilities, and skills are implicated in the struggle to survive: (1) access to a safe and secure habitation; (2) acquisition to strong genes; (3) altruism as revealed in kinship ties; and (4) linguistic competence.

Habitable Dwellings

Physical settings vary in resource distribution. Evolution favors a good fit between organism and environment. A great portion of earthly surfaces are not suitable for humans to flourish in dynamic states of abundance. Life is not located everywhere. The vast universe is a volatile, violent, expanse of toxic territory. Idle speculations about alien visitors from the dark corners of the universe are fodder for mindless chatter and science fiction. Planet Earth is located billions of light years away from verified life forms. It is uniquely suited for the cohabitation of living entities. Our physical surroundings inevitably impose their own assumptions on what social activities are able to make possible.

Striving subjects must adapt, at all times and in all ways, to constraints and obstacles in any habitable setting. Material conditions do not care one way or another. They are under no obligation to put back together what they tear apart. Greater sensitivity to the impact of our ecological situations may be a useful way to dispel false notions that human actors occupy center stage of their natural settings. What degrades the material world must also diminish human values just as well. Life-affirming values are necessary to promote unflinching regard for the sanctity of life, not just for the benefits of the rich and famous.

Large populations must be able to migrate away from harsh dangers or unsafe conditions. The ultimate goal is to achieve a state of harmony between nature and nurture. Ecological decay destroys not only population fitness but protection against extinction risks. Genetic fitness is able to improve procreative success and population diversity. On a molecular scale, chemical properties of protein protect against mutational incidents. On a system scale, biological organization favors health of organisms and population diversity. Excessive consumption of subsistence resources is no excuse for the depletion of nutritional needs; clean air, water, food, shelter, climate, and atmosphere.

Favorable settings enhance the capacity of a human community to adapt to multiple geographies and migrate across alien territory. Genetic fitness enhances odds of survival, fertility, and mating success. Intelligent life multiplies in direct proportion to direct access to the protective effects of a congenial atmosphere. Conversely, global health can be undermined by climate change, air pollution, fossil fuels, and disease. Health disparities are linked to higher mortality risks of lower educated citizens. Shorter life expectancy stems from diminished sense of future security.

Levels of a hopeless sense of future insecurity, contribute to loss of meaning and severe mortality risk. The presence or absence of safe and secure habitation helps to explain the difference between a robust or frail meaning system. A firm sense of place, refuge, affords protection from the cosmic storm. By implication, it is a mistake to locate 'personal meaning' within narrow confines of stable personality traits. A meaningful way of life is not simply the value of individual 'identity' but rather a closer fit between mortal 'existence' and 'ecological' habitability.

The meaning of survival is at stake. Life forces permeate all living creatures, who are also forces of life themselves. The ecological landscape provides protective cover for living organisms. Multiple pressures from nature and nurture must be withstood for territorial occupations to be secured. A surplus of material resources contributes to health and well-being in daily life. Human territories are vulnerable to environmental deterioration. What degrades earthly surfaces will ultimately degrade human valuations just as well. Without ecological protection, all living species would be reduced to dust.

Ruthless destruction of our earthly planet cannot be indefinitely prolonged. Natural instabilities aggravate wasteful consumption of finite resources and leave (relatively) powerless persons behind. Earthly resources are fragile and vulnerable to destruction. When reckless human beings desecrate their physical surroundings, they set into destructive motion what will ultimately destroy themselves. The law of habitation is inviolable. Robust ecological landscapes make human habitation possible and necessary. Territorial occupation and secure settlements are critical factors in mortality risks.

A strong sense of place has artistic value, along with historical and traditional artifacts, icons, and symbolic forms of representation. Fragmentations of settled habitats work in the opposite direction. Established customs, habits, routines, and styles break down in disruptive contexts of biodiversity loss. Life is sacred only if it is cherished as the ultimate value. It is desecrated insofar as inversive values are allowed to take its place. Sadly, ecological and humanitarian crises are intimately connected.

Timing is everything. Human beings are products rather than producers of time and place of birth and earthly conditions into which they are thrown. Life spans are prescribed, predetermined, at the beginning but not the middle or the end. The best predictor of a way of dying is a way of living that resides along the way. Much of the life course is programmed by genetic codes and modified by intentions and outcomes of social interaction. The legacy of succeeding generations is a composite expression of what the totality of what evolved inheritance makes manifest in reproductive success.

Claims of volition (free choice) are themselves shaped by the fact that striving subjects do not have full control over what resides 'inside' of their bodily boundaries (subconscious activation) or 'outsides' of external pressures (physical forces). The expanse of meaning systems, therefore, are not merely a dynamic product of the particulars of what we think or feel but rather by what inherited supplies of energy and matter determine the sheer inability of that we are not capable or willing to think or feel. Included activities bear the imprint of those are excluded from deliberate consideration.

Strong Genes

Favorable conditions and strong genes congeal together without fixed formula to sort out cause and effect. Genetic inscriptions do not produce uniform ways to generate useful meaning systems. Flesh and blood, skin and bones, do not talk back. Environment, meaning, and genes merge together, into integrated systems. Particulars do not exist in isolation as discrete elements but rather interact in collective form. Hence, there is no static 'self' or 'identity' that lurks in some hidden inner chamber.

What makes life worth living are the composite (additive) features of longevity, taken in relation to problematic behavior (subtractive) risks that shorten it. Similarly, the quality of existence is not assured by quantity. Optimal meanings are generated by the degree to which striving subjects are fully present to whatever is presented for labor intensive investments in creative inquiry. The wider world is open for attentive inspection from a changing slant of vantage points. A heuristic principle rules: use all there is to use. Make as much as possible with whatever possibilities are still open for inspection.

Genes contribute to whatever achieves evolutionary significance: reproduction, intelligence, competence, social cohesion, along with mutations, disease, disability, and health risks. Population survival depends on collective ability to adapt to mitigating constraints (unfavorable risks), overcome obstacles, and magnify opportunities. Genetic imprints are transmitted 'within' and 'across' generations of kinship ties. A small number of procreative successes tends to stabilize small population growth and reinforces conditions for long-term survival. Genetic compatibility is strengthened over long time periods as a consequence of robust selection and prevention of extinction. Diverse populations mix microorganisms together in complex ways to maximize reproductive success and improve the protective effects of the immune system.

Common genes are fluid, plastic, and expressive of wide variations in matters of organ regulation. Cell proliferations turn into neurons. Molecular compounds promote tissue formation in brain cells with tacit features. Genetic programs help to build a complex nervous system. Genetic complexity does not itself specify neural circuits which are inscribed as indirect features of multiple points of development in combined networks. Organ maintenance depends on the viability of microorganisms that interact in dynamic pathways of nutrition and defense against mutations. Chemical wiring of composite organization changes over time.

Therefore, reproductive success cannot be reduced to autonomic attributes of personality traits. Genetic features of sexual reproduction are not destiny. DNA conveys primitive instructions to build functional organs, not in a scaled down blueprint or map but rather as chemical compounds and material (informational) capacity. Birth signifies the success of an unfinished but viable human composition that is inseparable with the microorganisms with which everyone is interwoven.

General Intelligence

General intelligence (g) depends on the dynamic interplay of activated brain networks, modified levels and scales of organic autonomy. Feature detections access prior knowledge (memory), improve problem solving, support rapid information exchange, and preserve cognitive clarity at a global level. At no time or place are low level activations separate or detached from higher level computations. Small scale variations intersect with large scale means to preserve definition and direction. The genetic basis of inherited (potential) capacities and abilities promotes speed, efficiency, and adaption to difficult tasks and conflicting impediments. Gradual acquisition of broad conceptual ability is made possible by underlying substrata of specialized processes.

Hence, there is no organic separation between what is revealed on the surface of conscious awareness and what is concealed or revealed below (flesh and blood). Only folly is left to claim that self-awareness transcends material existence. When persons die, their self-awareness perishes with them. Distinctive features of human ingenuity require that competence and creativity are well integrated into intricate neurological networks of brain waves. What transpires above the neck is made possible what resides below the skull. Intelligence is not locked up in some higher chamber. Body language is intelligent too. No wonder that elevated levels of mind-body activation work together to enhance intrinsic measures of health, vitality, and tolerable levels of mortality risks.

General intelligence resonates in an active brain posed to make accurate inferences, implications, forecasts, and predictions about an indefinitely large number of possible outcomes. Hardwired genetic traits—including number, density, conductance, and velocity of molecular order—shape information processing capacity and shifting contours of general intelligence. Inertia is ruled out. The brain never sleeps. Anatomic cognitive systems, each of which exhibit acute sensitivities, are deeply integrated across broad distributions of intelligent applications.

Biology controls interact with broad states of neuronal development across the maturation process. Symbolic processes are imbedded in subconscious (non-symbolic) constructions (regularity, rules), general features (executive, memory), and developmental outcomes (sensitivity, stress) of immense cognitive variation. Molecular formats imply the coexistence of multiple levels, scales, and types of performative responses to external affordance. It is fortunate, therefore, that automatic, mechanical, and unintentional devices are left to perform so many invisible functions. Visible, observable forms of adaptation do not have to carry the full load of what transpires. Silent intelligence is a sanctuary, a refuge, from fake news and idle chatter.

The limits of general intelligence are open to controversy. One-size-fits-all models cannot be stretched in all directions at once. The world is a messy place. Intelligence does not exhaust the spectrum of human achievement. It is less leading to refer to striving subjects who happen to be intelligent than to make reference to intelligent persons. So much depends on what refined sensibilities are put to good use. Individual differences are simply too varied, complex, and intricate to measure acquired talent, persistence, and resolve, despite friction, strife, and strain that are neither welcome nor desirable.

The restless brain is a miniature model of the world. It does not take pictures or store copies but rather activates the best possible fit between intentions and effects of strategic behaviors. Stored knowledge, fluid and crystallized, favors pragmatic use. There are, however, no duplicate or copies of prior conditions, present constraints, or future opportunities. Spontaneous events only happen once.

Performative intelligence relies on flexible ability to solve novel tasks and move round obstacles and constraints. Conscious awareness conveys readiness to engage in logical reasoning tasks. Emotional intelligence is left to fill in the blanks. Spiritual inspiration transcends reason with faith. Subtle and intricate lines of demarcation between words and objects are useful in language acquisition, along with elevated verbal, emotional, and responsive sensibilities.

General intelligence accounts for much variation in diverse cognitive and affective abilities. It is largely heritable (40-60%), as expressed in brain tissue, molecular connectivity, and cell death. A portion of individual differences are due to genetic variability. Mutations are not to be discounted in the larger equation. Also relevant are links to psychotic disturbances and mental disorders. Brain power is a composite reflection of internal organizations that intersect with external factors to maximize reproductive success. Conversely, complex disturbances are known to partially account for organic disability. Risk factors are indirect reactions to environmental turbulence (depression and anxiety). It is futile to measure intelligent capacities in a social vacuum.

Physical pressures are imposed on body surfaces. Hence, pathogenic outcomes, are part of the larger, mixed equation. Malleable features shift across two levels of activation; upward toward growth, health, and ascendance (high IQ) or downward toward atrophy, illness, and descent (low IQ). Intelligence conveys no fixed effects. It can be nurtured (preserved) or abused (destroyed). Access to a safe dwelling or secure habitation enables striving subjects to nurture and protect their genetic heritage. Conversely, intelligent achievements can easily be squandered through prolonged exposure to misuse and abuse.

The so called 'body-mind' problem amounts to little more than pure fiction. The same liability applies to a nature-nurture dualism. Human beings are constituted (biologically) and constructed (socially) as synthetic, integrated, and wholistic entities. It makes no sense to carve up body, mind, and spirit into separate compartments. Nor is it feasible to leave either matter or energy out of an animated equation. False appeal to mind without matter are just as invidious (counter-factual) as the other way around.

IQ tests are given to 'individuals' and scored 'individually' in research centers that are detached from the reality of daily life. IQ can reinforce false notions, namely that smart test takers are solely responsible for their lofty test scores. Left out is attention to constrains (stark reality of daily life) that impact on test taking ability. Intelligence registers in social interactions, communicative networks, large institutions, democratic deliberations, to say nothing of the transitory status of fame and fortune. Smart people maintain selective access to smart people who share elevated levels of competence and compatibility and decisively, they chose to live in conditions of isolation and detachment from less articulate members of society. Advantaged persons magnify their collective advantages with one another, just as disadvantaged persons struggle to cope with their shared disadvantages.

Displays of exceptional talents are not uniformly translated from exemplary modes of general intelligence. Cognitive skills are relatively narrow when compared with a wider array of inspiring talents, to say nothing of integrity of character or fidelity to duty. Practice and preparation inform artistic merit: musical, poetic, discursive, artistic, aesthetic, technological and heroic displays of exemplary conduct. IQ scores do not afford convincing explanations for what moves dedicated persons to obey a higher calling, including sacrifice and suffering for the sake of others,

Irony. Unintelligent views of intelligent have caused great damage to the universality of human dignity and intrinsic worth. It does not make common sense to confuse the totality of what makes life worth living with ugly inscriptions of superior or inferior classes of world population. A century of advances in brain science has been ruthlessly confiscated and exploited to afford rationalistic justification for civilian casualties from brutal military invasions, genocide, ethnic cleansing, racism, sexism, denegation of immigrants (rapists, criminals), and subordination of innocent women and children. The slaughter of millions of victims during two World Wars was infiltrated with hysteric rhetoric—as cause to wipe 'inferior' populations off the face of the earth so the purity of 'superior' classes could cling to their privileged positions. A greater truth must not be displaced. Variations in general intelligence can be undermined by malignant forces of greed, corruption, lies, and deceptions that lie that heart of human maladies. There is an urgent need to galvanize cultural resistance to intelligent ignorance with the redemptive force of restorative justice.

Kinship Ties

Life is presumptive. It can be taken for granted or rendered meaningless. Take the easy way out. Follow the course of least resistance. Go through the motions. Pretense seeks refuge. Nothing matters. Struggle seems futile. Withdraw into passivity: idle, listless, without aim, direction, or purpose. Feign indifference to what happens to others. Most people are more trouble than they are worth. Detachment follows: inattention, distraction, inertia. The grim reality of daily life will be over shortly. Give in. Give up. Resign. Retreat. Don't bother to care one way or another. Once the damage is done, further struggle is a waste of time. A pervasive sense of futility is all that remains. Bare living rarely beats living at all.

A larger implication follows. Mortal existence may be grounded in physical reality but it is still fluid and malleable. In a fast-changing world, nothing stays the same for very long. Lack of predictability and predictability reside side-by-side. Meaning systems are linguistic products of discursive use which can lapse into misuse and abuse. Animated meanings, therefore, are passively deconstrued the same way they are actively constructed. Gains are subject to loss.

Positive signs mingle with negative signs. What makes things better may also make them worse. Valuations are vulnerable to devaluation. Credit does not prevent discredit. What matters (ultimately, urgently) to one striving subject may not matter (least or not at all) to someone else. Arbitrary and fabricated meaning systems may prevail episodically, systemically, or last a life time. Life gives only what it can take away.

The point is not to underscore the relativity of all things. It is rather to caution against presumptions of linguistic sovereignty. Words and things do not cling together, like cement or glue. These cautions may lead to greater appreciation of what resides at the other end of an imprecise scale. Altruism is a powerful force that does not yield easily to a downward tug. It is an intrinsic feature in kinship ties that must struggle to withstand the brute force of conflicts and contradictions in human bonds. The concept of 'altruism' is simple to define in abstract terms. What registers is regard for the welfare of others. The notion of 'other' does not imply mere object (as objectified in academic discourse) but rather an alternative source of relevance. Subjects and situations are fully implicated. Egocentric impulses are not always impediments.

A brute fact: human beings are the most altruistic species on the planet. Only literate organisms possess the capacities, abilities, and skills to establish strong, resilient bonds with one another. Mortal regard for collective life serves as an active baseline. Applied language use strives to tolerate confusion, conflict, and contradiction. Social interactions align with vested interests and partisan alliances. If striving subjects were not subject to mortality risks, there would be no need for altruistic values to arise in the first place. Fortunately, altruistic impulses do not have to hear the full weight of human burdens. Benevolence, compassion, gratitude and other tender mercies help to alleviate stress and strains in strategic activities.

A heuristic principle, a goodness of fit (between organism and environment) promotes an altruistic goal and standard by which affectionate displays register as either appropriate (relevant) or inappropriate (irrelevant) in shared pursuit of collective goals. A decision-making principle rules. Amicable subjects are able to pursue reproductive outcomes, shared identities, intangible benefits, including intimacy, cohesion, or ties that bind. What benefits others indirectly (eventually) may increase direct benefits (immediately) to the care giver.

In a moral equation, the appearance of altruism may confer added value to identity or self-esteem. If so, it pays to be an altruist, due to wider latitudes of interdependence, when compared with non-altruists who use independent, subversive or coercive measures of constraint. Pressure to move away from egoistical motives allow altruistic persons to determine how to assist others more quickly with less reliance on deeper resources of mindfulness, focus, and attention. Kinship ties are strengthened by shared engagement in rituals and routines that are collectively valued, highly varied.

Highly varied meaning systems are built upon, and diversified, from rich biological substrata.

Altruism appeals to collective values of a shared community. Behaviors benefit others, even when risk entails sacrifice. There may be costs of reductions of givers' welfare. Pain, trauma, and suffering are worthy causes of intervention. Altruistic motives contribute to the wider search for what makes striving subjects to grow, flourish, and become richly human. Kinship ties are critical.

Genetic relations favor strong ties among family and friends. Natural selection favors altruistic displays on derived benefits of social support and helping behavior as worthy of derived costs.

When costs exceed benefits, helping behavior is subject to diminished returns. Since harmful behaviors are also core features of moral systems, selfless and selfish impulses must be reconciled in due time. Kinship ties confer fitness benefits to their progeny. The flow of altruistic generosity does not expand in a straight line of progressive or regressive modification. Instead, congenial actions must align with congenial values to maximize benefits over costs.

In general, family members are more altruistic to each other, due to natural selection, than to more distant friends, where altruistic exchanges require higher degrees of reciprocity. Family ties promote emotive closeness, proximity, frequent contact, and shared history. Kinship has the most direct effect on altruistic members, whereas friendships are dependent on relational quality and prior reciprocity. Altruism fades in relation to social distance, remote location, social isolation, and infrequent contact. Diminished returns, changed by natural selection, enable mixed outcomes to dissolve into a stable equilibrium between selfish and selfless motives rather than the elimination of one over the other.

Kinship ties are vulnerable to freeloaders and defectors of a united cause. Another qualification follows. If small groups favor minority interest, and large groups favor majority priorities, altruistic preferences may be cut short. Risks may exceed costs. Selfish impulses favor lack of reciprocity. Selfless urges favor costly measures of reciprocity. If there are no costs, there is no reason for altruistic appeals. Helping acts, in accord with ethical standards, aid those in distress. Altruism declines in cases of those who are located at greater distances from local sites cites of generous affection. Empathy increases overlap in neural responses of self and other. Feelings of cohesion are clearly observable in kinship ties based on shared history, close relations, strong affection, and geographical proximity. Reproductive success rewards fitness benefits.

Benevolence signifies a desire to be good, kind, or chartable. Malevolence signifies a disposition of ill will. The troubles of others are magnified when socially undesirable factors enter desirable equations. The virtue of benevolence not only transcends malignant dispositions but also aligns with deliberate will to care about the welfare of struggling persons and perform acts on their own behalf. Malevolence, in contrast, attempts to alleviate inward, private pain by dispersing chronic discomfort on the backs of others who are expected to bare the greater bunt of societal maladies. Malevolence gains traction by construing opponents, rivals, and aliens as solely responsible for their own (self-imposed) misery. Vicarious victimization, scapegoating, and crude stereotypes are symbols of misattributed guilt and shame.

Summary

Appreciation for mortal existence acquires significance for striving subjects who value their distinctive place in the wider scheme of things. Access to favorable conditions increases human sensitivity of coveted valuations across the life span. An abiding sense of dignity and worth may strengthen personal resolve to invest in a higher calling that transcends solitary preoccupation with a narrow range of vested interests. The ultimate test of living well is actualized in being fully present in the flux and flow of daily events. Favorable conditions are fully manifest to striving subjects who struggle to maintain direct access to a safe and secure source of protective habitation. Reckless, careless exploitation of earthly surfaces sets in motion massive destruction of human settlements and material abundance. Genes, identity, and setting must be carefully aligned to magnify productive conditions for members of a common community to live together in close bonds of cohesion and solidarity. General intelligence is a personal acquisition but socially distributed. Kindship ties magnify the strength of altruistic outcomes but diminish with social distance and impersonal detachment.

3

Affirmative Activities

It does not pay to take life for granted. A life worth living is worth the price. Still, ideal standards can be elusive. There is no firm way for optimal conditions to be put in place. Solemn resolutions rarely last till death does us part. Cherished notions can be defeated. Beliefs and opinions are fleeting and transitory. Meaning systems are fluid and malleable rather than fixed or rigid. No worthy goal is immune to change. Nothing stays the same for very long. What registers as significant one moment may fade into insignificance the next. Values are arbitrary. Facts are open to dispute. Risks are unavoidable. Uncertainty not ruled out. Ambiguity clouds the way. Life does not unfold in a straight line.

Reasonable claims do not preclude unreasonable outcomes. The best of intentions may lead to the worst of outcomes. Aspirations appear worthy or honorable until unmitigated pain and suffering takes a toll. Unbearable burdens eliminate odds of compensation. Time does not heal all wounds. Irreversible loss owes no comfort to recoverable gain. By implication, a life worth living is neither inevitable nor immune to subversive setbacks, even when idealized aims are within our grasp. For tentative reasons, positive affirmations restore faith in reaching higher ground. It is naïve to assume there is a clear path to achieve exceptional progress toward a brighter future.

Affirmations are intrinsic features of credible meaning. Preparation and practice are preparations for skilled performance. Stress and strain are tensions to be tolerated, withstood or overcome. It is not realistic to invoke a straight path up or down. Early failure predicts later success. Short term losses may lead to a greater resolve to defeat impediments to goal directed aims.

Positive gains do not cancel out negative intrusions. Right and wrong comingle as a lingering theme. The search for affirmative valuations may give rise to questions about ultimate concerns. It takes resolute struggle to locate restorative actions in relief of turbulent or troubled times. Conflicted realities may be too messy to be resolved in a straight line. In life, there are no friction free territories to conquer but only entangled paths.

Core Values

It is difficult to envision a good life without a rich surplus of strong affirmations. Validations permeate the social fabric. Positive appraisals assign merit or worth to personal aspirations. At issue are values of importance, relevance. Activity confirms validation of core values. Assigned facts are value-laden. Interpretations are persuasive. Affirmative activities must be reality tested in public settings if they are to prevail in credible form. Striving subjects assign importance to cherished clams and strive to defend them.

Critical values are guiding principles in daily life. Affirmative outcomes afford tacit motives for personal strivings and social aspirations. Valued priorities are not mere products of subjective judgments. Evaluative judgments serve as implicit guides for concerted behavior to be taken as desirable, tolerable, forbidden, or unobtainable. Core values are at risk in contested aspects of public performance.

At stake are relative merits of creative inquiry: why we value personal knowledge; why we approve of shared intelligence; why we seek insightful exchanges of alternative meanings; why we discredit or devalue alternative value systems that appear foreign or alien to our own. Similarities are easier to reconcile than differences. Applied knowledge acquires direct verification of shared interests. Affirmative validations are likely to promote congenial actions, strong attachments, and collective alignments of alternative meaning systems.

Core values—respect, honesty, and trust—are critical measures of optimal human encounters. Taken together, they congeal into aggregates modes of credibility, merit, and validation. Across diverse public settings, respect ranks highest. Most decisive is due regard for the integrity of others. Even slight displays of disrespect are well known to invalidate personal identity and social integrity. Respectful validation is rooted in principles of separation and tolerance of uncertainty. It also serves as an antidote to frustration. Repeated disturbance leads to detachment, low self-esteem, and social distance. Mutual affirmations evolve into an internal norm. Close bonds magnify the salience of congruent value systems. Cohesive exchanges provide symbolic protection against humiliating displays and contemptuous tactics in conflict situations. Self-respect qualifies as a basic condition of social valuation. Mutual affirmations of shared respect are selective, exclusionary, and distinctive. Elaborated displays of collective regard are a stabilizing force and intricate principle of moderation.

When people express themselves in a respectful manner, other things seem to fall into place. When viewed as a sign of admiration and regard, a state of mutual respect is most often taken as a precondition for other types of constructive value. Activated respect qualifies as a core value and a cherished virtue as well. The style in question is rarely taken for granted as a presumption or entitlement. Multiple references construe persons as distinct individuals; for varied modes of expressive or interpretive response. Once in place, striving subjects typically view mutual respect as a great virtue and source of intrinsic merit.

Public displays of shared respect give rise to a wide array of secondary associations; really caring about one another; revealing an attitude of sincerity, openness, tolerance, and trust in others' thoughts, feelings, beliefs, morals, priorities, interests, judgments, and tastes. Fringe benefits include a heightened sense of social support for the pursuit of diverse needs and wants. Praise, advice, judgment, and criticism are given freely and taken in an appropriate spirit. Also relevant are collective need to explore unresolved difficulties, issues, and problems in a more depth and detail that would otherwise be possible.

Respect for persons aligns with honesty in discourse. It involves the willingness to speak and listen openly before others. The value of honesty is linked to a larger array of negotiated discoveries. After all, a person may respect another for reasons that have little to do with the way these subjects interact with each other. Honest exchanges contribute to a rich legacy of shared knowledge. An honest speaking style is manifest in clear, detailed, and complex accounts of real-life events. It may take a great deal of honest effort to construe contested matters from other's views and try for others to see things from one's own unique perspective. Brutal honesty may have an adverse side effect. Honest effort to tell significant others what they are not prepared or willing to hear is likely to cause hurt feelings that are covered over in ways that inhibit protracted honesty in future encounters. Sometimes frank messages arrive before or too later for messengers to deal with them.

Respect for persons leads to greater regard for honesty in dialogue and trust in relational integrity. Trust qualifies as the third most highly regarded value, in part because trust can operate well outside the narrow confines of human encounters. If respect is taken as a cherished value, and honesty is a labor-intensive outcome, then trustful acts qualify as soft and fragile. The reason is that trust does not have to be subject to shared validation. A trusting person can believe in the strength, ability, or integrity of anyone or anything of intrinsic merit. Trust emerges in distinctive patterns. Not only does it signal a stance of confidence and good will, but it also constitutes an intangible resource for negotiation or regeneration.

Mutual trust and shared commitment facilitate acts of self-verification, which in turn lead to positive conceptions of personal identity, as well as more generous valuations of others. High-trust persons defend their sense of optimum and conviction about the integrity of their relational bonds against the press of external sources of risk and threat. Low-trust persons, in contrast, often amplify adverse implications of outsiders' negative behavior and ignore constructive inferences about the possibility of positive actions. Personal trust is evaluated along broad dimensions of accommodation, interdependence, commitment, and readiness to sacrifice for the sake of the welfare of valued persons.

Respect, honesty, and trust work together to promote solidary and cohesion in egalitarian relations. However, these core values, individual or collective, are vulnerable to exploitation. Devaluations of disrespect, dishonesty, and disrespect are common maladies, particularly in unfavorable conditions where deception and deprivations are taken as manipulative advantages. Deprivation and demoralization signify inability to cope, deprivation of spirit, weakness, atrophy, or distress. It is important, therefore, to recognize that core values are two-sided devices to assign credit or discredit, value or devalue, worth or unworthy, to all manner of human encounters.

Mismatched value systems are troublesome. They contribute to discord, hurt, and upset feelings. Inability or unwillingness to take unspoken signals into account may lead to an impasse or irreconcilable differences that are not amenable to resolution. When incongruent values are placed on too many things, there is apt to be tension, stress, annoyance, irritation, confusion, and struggle in misguided efforts to iron them out. There may also be a sense that social agents are from different worlds or embrace different realities. Friction, strife, and strain makes it more difficult to translate back and forth from one value system to another.

With no way out of protracted difficulties, and no options or better methods of translation back and forth, a case of linguistic gridlock is likely to be deeply ingrained with no relief in sight. These reservations are necessary remainders that the affirmative value of core values, while intrinsically valuable, are not to be taken for granted as a firm presumption or conflated sense of entitlement. Affirmative mechanisms that facilitate the close alignment of divergent core values, when misused, abused, or ignored, may also be inverted, turned upside down, replace short-term gains with long-term loss.

Fallible Standards

It is an open question whether the promise of a life well lived is available to everyone. Mere existence does not qualify. Nor is it mandatory to recognize one's place in the larger scheme of things. Not everyone possesses the vigor and vitality to pursue the best of intentions. Physical forces may overwhelm social influence. Inhabitable stressors may also stand in the way. Strong ties are not always available to marginal citizens. Favorable conditions require resource allocation.

Genetic liabilities and intellectual disabilities are difficult to overcome. Disease prevails over ease. Kindship ties erode in broken homes. Child neglect and abuse diminish adult options. Altruism deteriorates along the way. Poverty does not prevent a protracted state of impoverishment. Lack of social mobility undermines faith in struggle for a better way of life. Affirmation affords no assurance of protection from disaffection. Core values can be tossed upside down.

These precautions are necessary to defend realistic standards over idealistic substitutes. What transpires matters far more than what could, should, might, or ought to take place. Without empirical standards to measure the distance between constraint and opportunity, anything goes and nothing is ruled out.

Mechanisms of compensation are available to striving subjects who are motivated to live the best way of life imaginable.

Each active, vital human being retains an intrinsic interest in make common, salient, and realistic sense of contested public settings. It is one thing to merely imagine the best conditions for human beings to survive, prosper, mature, and flourish. It is quite another to live a vital way of life for the sake of what each life makes possible before others. Baseline conditions must be satisfied for human encounters to bring out the best of everyone and minimize the worst. Brief involvements in episodic engagements can easily fulfill merger standards of impression management. Routine tasks do not count for much credit or credibility.

Reality testing activity can be assessed against two radically different types of paradigmatic evaluation. On a local level, vague presumptions of infallibility may arise from intuitively appealing notions of what transpires in a complex public sphere as being somehow free of error, mistake, falsehood, or deception. Infallible subjects may presume to know everything there is to know about a given subject. On a regional scale, competing groups may produce "true believers" who presume their distinctive worldviews to be infinitely superior to any alternative conception available on a human scale. Zealous advocates proclaim one certain way as the only possible way to seek ultimate truth, wisdom, or glory worthy of emulation and worship with resolute conviction. On a global scale, a devote condition of sacred infallibility may be collectively attributed to some higher force, a supreme being, a god, or the cosmos, as defined in abstract theological terms.

Worship of a higher power implicates firm belief in a supreme being with infinite capacity to know all things, hear all things, see all things, and reveal all things to finite human beings through an infallible method of divine revelation. Sacred invocations may be infused or imbued with spiritual force, magical power, and resolute conviction in timeless truth, beyond further change or subsequent alteration. Paradox: claims of changeless truth arise in a changing world. Sweeping claims and inerrant dogma seek to transcend all manner of doubt. The appealing notion of eternal revelation may be a source of primordial comfort in precarious or troubled times for the faithful who can imagine or envision their own lives as being subject to a theological master plan. True believers are free to worship at the sacred throne of faith which passes all human understanding. Thereby, the finite limits of mortal existence are elevated into a transcendent domain of infinite, eternal truth.

Illusions of infallibility interfere with the modest ability to recognize or even admit to the possibility of holding a mistaken belief about the world at large. The wide variety of errors and miscues affect the veracity of what we say and do before others. Conflations of superiority rule out the larger potential value of repeated testing for errors, miscues, and mistakes, both as a means of further discovery and as a rational for devising new tests or subsequent refinements in reality-testing procedures to gain a better understanding of anomalous, incomplete, idealized or misdirected efforts in complex goal attainment.

Early sociologists once thought the demise of religious doctrines, coupled with the rise of science, would lead to the ascendance of secular ideology. They were wrong. It turns out that billions of people who struggle to survive on a precarious and dangerous planet simply cannot exist without comfort of a timeless promise of eternal security. Much of the religious violence in the 21st century owes to a singular claim found in all major religious traditions, namely the superiority of one definition of God (sacred documents) along with inferior definition of alternative conceptions. Therefore, holy wars are justified to punish infidels who refuse to be converted to an alternative paradigm of theological indoctrination.

Contemporary religious vengeance can be fortified by those who prefer to look back to doctrines of ancient religious as alternative to the stark methods of scientific inquiry. The stark clash between sacred and secular outlooks also registers in the value-laden tendency of some persons to organize their cherished valuations according to a master plan of "redemption" and "contamination" of moral, ethical, and aesthetic overtones. Redemption transforms bad into good. Contamination transforms good into bad.

Invocations of purity and impurity are widely dispersed across wide spectrums of technical civilization. Also relevant are historic and cultural traditions that become more complicated over vast time periods. Singular appeal to simple purity and complex impurity account for a great deal of cultural turbulence that either seeks refuge in a regressive return to simpler times or places more weight on progressive changes in an ever more complicated world where no one knows everything about anything and no one gets in the last world or can be located as a final authority. Globalization, technology, artificial intelligence, robotics, and wired world bring humanity together and separate national ideology and class distinctions at the same time.

Metaphoric linkages work together to transpose notions of infallibility, perfection, and purity into close alignment. The distinction between infallibility and fallibility gains traction in another selective illusion. Utopian fantasies or mortal beings are idealized as a means to achieve a state or condition of "perfect communication" with one another. When judged by a standard of redemption over contamination (malignant forces), a superior performance maybe defined in positive, elevated, and rarified terms. When judged by a standard of contamination over redemption (impure forces), an inferior performance may be defined in negative, lower, fallen and deteriorated terms.

By implication, comparative standards qualify as personal constructs based on inflated ascriptions and deflated attributes; credit or discredit, valuation or devaluation, qualification or disqualification. An awe-inspiring vision of perfect communication activates a lofty vision of a transparent world without visible signs of misinterpretation, miscommunication, or misunderstanding (problematic talk). Words magic may be sufficient to desire that everyone could somehow express themselves clearly and interpret others accurately, without a hint of noise, distortion, disruption, of interference.

Perfectionism makes matters worse. Extreme striving for flawless performance may infiltrate all aspects of daily life. Failure is avoided at all costs. Mistakes imply deficits. Relentless aspirations to achieve exceptional performance also compensates for hidden deficiencies. Perfect urges may be directed toward the self, as exhibited in unobtainable standards, doubts about achievements, excessive concern over troubles, and hyper-criticism. Perfectionistic urges may also be attributes to others as revealed in false assumptions that other impose high standards on oneself. Perfectionist motives may be misattributed to society at large, as judged to be solely responsible for personal and social inability to satisfy prevailing performative standards.

Resources, abilities, and skills must all be amenable to rigorous test. A great deal of dedication, preparation, and practice is required to perform at a distinctive level of health and well-being. What qualifies is a striving subject who achieves merited status or rank, judged as worthy of honorific emulation before others. Infallible, perfectionistic, flawless achievements are neither necessary nor obtainable. Instead, make the most of whatever possibilities are available to stand the test of time.

Positivity and negativity are not mutually exclusive. What matters is the surplus of production at either end of the scale. Brief episodes of negative display will still leave room for some measure of adaption, order, duty, discipline, and deliberation. Professional competition rewards dedication, discipline, and determination, to win at all costs. In effect, resilient perfectionism still applies—many are called, few are chosen. Conversely, maladaptive perfectionism follows from standards beyond reach, impossible goals, and personal worth measured exclusively in terms of exceptional performance.

The degree of perfectionism depends on vulnerability, hazard, and risk. Clinical maladies surface: lack of pleasure from labor-intensive tasks; unrealistic aspirations; tension and anxiety; all-or-nothing concepts; intolerable gaps between existing performances and ultimate standards. Extreme perfectionism turns out to be far less perfect than willingness to tolerate imperfection—confidence in the best that one can be. Sometimes conflated notions of winning or losing end up mattering more than the intrinsic value of collective participation itself.

It is important for exceptional achievers to know the difference between a lifetime of longing for perfection and the quest of excellence. Vulnerability increases on several fronts at once; dichotomous notions of success and failure; appeal to absolute standards that leave no room for suboptimal outcomes; indulgence in major attribution errors in a global tendency to envision self, others, and society as cause or reason for the prevention of achieving superior status or rank. Left out of the explanation is sheer ignorance of the larger scheme of things. No promise of a master category is available to guide our way through darkness and light, illness and health, vitality of youth and decay of age. Mortal forgetfulness stands in the way.

Utopian flight into perfection, infallibility, and purity are risky standards to impose on daily events. It does not matter whether perfectionistic, infallible, or purified notions are predicated on intervention (revelation) or exceptional measures of ideological success (achievement). When strategic rivals are accountable to flawless performances, they set themselves to struggle in vain against what amount to implausible standards of aspirations, expectations, or goals. There must be greater provision, therefore, for honoring a distinction between what can be subject to falsification and what cannot be settled one way or another.

Adherents of fallibilism, imperfection, and impurity need to learn from mixed blessings of lived experiences and to distinguish between better and worse claims to know this or that about one thing or another. If we as human beings qualify as fallible, imperfect, impure creatures, we should, as rational agents, acknowledge this fallibility and treat ourselves and others accordingly. Also relevant is the need to replace negative and degraded attributions with compensative measures of positive affirmations and reasonable expectations. Sometimes the desire to make things better matters less than resolute ability to keep them from getting worse.

Positive Affections

The quest for what makes life worth living cannot be specified in abstract terms. Nor is it clear how to be fully present, overcome obstacles, seize opportunities, acquire discipline, or fulfill ultimate desires. There is no master plan, universal code, or prescriptive formulas, for secular deliverance. Reliance on authority does not lead to the highest authority. There is no magical source to tell us who we are, what we should do, how we might act, to make things right or correct for wrong. Only by access to creative inquiry are promises to be kept and gains to be secured: turn confusion into clarity; darkness into light; ignorance into insight. No mandates are available to guide struggling subjects to the promised land. Nothing of value is universally valued. Truth does not rule out lie. Deception is everywhere to be found. The only way to know right from wrong is to test the difference and act accordingly.

The urge to take things for granted only works until it cannot be taken for granted anymore. The wider world all to easily passes us by. Nothing stays the same for long. Disruptive change means it takes less and less time for more to happen. Core values, however cherished, are subject to inversion, or turned upside down, at any time. What starts to work well may work out badly later on. Fallible standards provide fleeting comfort but not from total discomfort, irreversible loss.

Idealism is no substitute for realism. It takes hard work to know what to be or how to act in a precarious world that leaves too many disturbed persons by the wayside. Odds do not favor disadvantaged persons who cannot defend themselves or speak on behalf of their own vested interests. Social immobility gives rise to fixed entrapment. Informed desires for (upward) ascendance are vulnerable to (downward) descendance for those who cannot find their own way.

Despites these grim reminders, direct access to a rich surplus of positive affection can still lead the way to a brighter day. Mutual affections are a powerful way to offset the unaffectionate effects of their complementary opposites. The intensity, salience, and impact of positive affect will be, on average, much less intense than for collective effects of negative affect. A same imbalance holds for multiple tensions: validation-invalidation, acceptance-rejection, or gain-loss. For these reasons, affective exchanges are highly valued, not just as a way to deal with trials and tribulations, but rather in spite of their adverse impact.

The need for affection is an intrinsic drive. Surface displays activate deeper rewards. Affectionate exchanges are desired for benefits to their partners. Personality traits intersect with interactive states. Emotional strategies are designed to keep valued relations active, preserve desired ends, reinforce satisfaction, and in good repair. Positive emotions are distinctive and cluster into closely aligned attributes. Positive emotions activate expressions of love, care, joy, happiness, interest, and excitement. Negative emotions activate expressions of anger, fear, and sadness. Affections enhance shared (positive-sum) power, mutual attractions (like-love), and mutual engagement (ego-involvement). Conversely, disaffections activate individual (zero-sum) power, disaffiliation (dislike-hate), and shared detachment (disinterest). In effect, shared powers, positive emotions, and mutual engagement can work together to maintain a stable state of temperance and moderation. Conversely, lack of affection tends to produce egocentric power, dislike, distain, or hate, distance and detachment.

Narrative themes favor multiple displays of mutual affections. Following accounts were derived from affectionate relations where a surplus of working agreement and mutual understanding prevailed.

Note: S stands for source and O stands for object of exchange relations.

Loving Agreement

S/O believe in things so dear yet so inexplicable—like true love. S/O listen at all times, keep an open mind, and show unconditional love. S/O have talked about everything—politics, morals, love for Madison, fun and pain. S/O find that comfort shown out of love is easier than when confronted for some other reason. S/O make passionate love or share their troubles. S/O can always reach a compromise—they have mutual trust, love and a strong commitment to one another. S/O share nothing but a spirit of love between them. S/O comfort one another and both react in a very caring and loving manner. S/O share unconditional love, devotion, and mutual willingness to help any way possible without asking why. S/O share a strong bond—if either one is in trouble, the other will always be there to express love despite everything. S/O get along no matter what; they talk about agreeable ideas because they love each other so much—they can talk about everything: men, cooking, catty women, politics, money, health, future goals, morals, sex, and the weather. S/O find that walking into the apartment is like coming home; they are able to catch up quickly; conversation begins with their own concerns and expands to include other relations, past and present; when the phone rings, neither one will answer if they are actively talking—if one is thirsty, the other will bring a drink; likewise, if necessary, one will change a disc, pack bowl of pot or tie a shoe; there is utmost respect and care that has grown steadily over the last eight years.

Note: core values are located across a wide expanse of sense-making practices: comfort, concern, trust, care, devotion, and respect for topics large and small. Troubles are shared in an amicable spirit. Each partner can talk about everything or anything, without a need for defense from negative judgement. Creative meanings multiply when open minds are able to use words and gestures without fear of negative reprisals. Distinctions between like and dislike provide weak indicators of mutual attraction. Distinctions between love and hate are much stronger indicators of the sheer magnitude of mutual attraction.

The search for love and intimacy is risky, of course. Acts of manipulation, calculation, betrayal, neglect, or abandonment are not to be discounted. For the majority of young adults, however, promise outweighs hazards. Intimate exchanges enable caring partners to feel alive, fresh, vital, loved, cared for, listened to, and revered in return. Expansive themes of opportunity abound; one loves to agree, one agrees to love; and one loves to agree and agrees to love at the same time. Loving agreements are manifest in common striving for states of proximity, closeness, playfulness, and mutual touching. There is ample provision for collaboration, support, intimate topics, secret codes, and improvised idioms where much is grasped with a tacit, intuitive and unspoken sense of shared history.

Likeable Agreement

S/O like to encourage each other. S/O like to pick up on the good stuff right away. S/O like the same music, movies, fancy dinners, plays, and hang out. S/O like to poke fun at other friends and have fun doing it—sometimes it is great fun to gang up on other people. S/O like to spend time together; they seem to agree about everything. S/O like karate, pool, tennis, basketball, and belief in God. S/O share qualities of kindness and generosity, like the same sports, share similar views, and love to joke around and act crazy and goofy. S/O can tell each other everything; other people tell them that they are so much alike that other people cannot tell them apart. S/O like making agreements because it is like a support system, building up confidence with each other; when they disagree, they are like lawyers trying to prove a point and get the others' approval. S/O help each other, give positive reinforcement, look at the world in a similar way, like the same music, enjoy exercise, and love piano—it is clear that they agree about most everything. S/O are so alike that it is almost scary; they work as a team when talking with other people; they play off each other, love to joke around, and be sarcastic; they are always up for something; S draws the line in the exact same place that O does.

Core values of kindness, generous, support, and help are directed, more than any other narrative style, toward leisure activities, fun, and games. Here what they 'like' to do are favored pastimes that are not taken seriously. Likeable and enjoyable acts of affection depend on the values of moods, beliefs, and attitudes used as framing devices to start or stop working on a shared plan, objective, or goal. There is a playful spirit that features more than enough laugher, joking, kidding, and banter to go around. Likable and enjoyable encounters afford psychic protection against the corrosive effects of wear and tear, stress and strain. What is so striking is how the slant of active voices, blended identities, and engaging subject matter appear so life affirming. There is open provision for reaffirmation and renewal of strong bonds between kindred spirits. Likeable agreements are attractive because they are often so generous, expansive, inclusive, pervasive, and forgiving for all manner of slights and miscues.

Enjoyable Agreement

S/O enjoy everything together because they have the same interests and deep personal concerns. S/O enjoy hearing what the other has to say—they ask as many questions as possible. S/O enjoy a close friendship where neither one is motivated by what can be gained from the other. S/O enjoy ways that they can give to each other— it makes for healthy and enjoyable relations. S/O enjoy making fun—each one antagonizes the other, laughing, joking all the time. S/O enjoy the same things, stay pretty calm, and do not let little things bother them. S/O enjoy sitting in the sun, as well as playing games just for fun, with no competition, such as pool. S/O enjoy teasing or making fun without offending or hurting anyone's feelings. S/O enjoy inside jokes, sitting, talking about nothing, and laughing. Note: mentions of enjoyment do not mention core values. Instead, the multiple pleasures of enjoyment are a reminder. Shared affections do not have to be intense or charged in order to be effective. Nothing is gained by calculation or manipulation. Conversation flows without coercion, manipulation, or power struggles. Stay calm. Don't get little things get in the way. Don't take things too seriously. Make fun. Joke around. Laugh a lot.

Happy Agreement

S/O know what makes each other happy. S/O know each other well and can make each other happy or angry with equal ease. S/O share a strong sense of give-and-take—they have a great system of finding ways to keep them both happy. S/O talk about the very things that make each of them sad, happy, mad, or anything else—they often blurt things out and interrupt each other also. S/O are open and honest with each other, knowing that each will accept and understand anything the other has to say; whether it be a helping hand in a job search or sending the other a small gift in the mail; they both work to help each other succeed and be happy.

Happiness is recognizable, a pleasant spirit, a spontaneous manner, a contagion that is at once expansive, reinforcing, and wholly or partially reciprocated, with lots of smiling, interest, excitement, and joy seen as active and energetic striving that can be displayed or revealed before others. Measures of happiness are not easily calculated in terms of a zero-sum game, where the more for you, the less for me: and the happier you get, the sadder it makes me feel. To the contrary. Public displays of mutual happiness fit better into a positive-sum equation where the more for you, the more for me, and the more for us, the more for others too. A spirit of happiness and joy is an antidote to hostility in conflict situations with potential for cruelty.

Caring Agreement

S/O care very much about the well-being of one another. S/O feel a sense of security knowing the other will care to hear one's own problems. S/O get along so well on many issues because they both have a caring nature. S/O care about each other's well-being—it makes their friendship very strong. S/O listen with attentive, caring, empathetic eyes and direct focus on one another. S/O know how to comfort each other—they are extremely caring and supportive. S/O hear each other; their reactions are caring, understanding, and motherly. S/O let each other know they care with words or actions (gifts, surprise, visits, etc.).

Care favors sharing, empathy, comfort, support, security, problem solving. A tender speaking/listening style reveals shared regard for personal well-being. Aesthetic features of love, care, and concern are remarkably similar in texture and tone. The is a pervasive, all-embracing spirit at work in unspoken signs of reassurance or admiration. Sights and sounds resemble a collective celebration. It is one thing to be imbued with an abiding sense of love, care, and concern for the of a specific person. It is another thing to be reveal affectionate regard for each member of aligned community. People who care about themselves help others to care about each other. There is pleasure in the shared construction of a living text.

Exciting Agreement

S/O use slang and jargon mixed with excitement and laugher. S/O are very talkative and use expressive body language whenever they get excited. S/O get along well and get excited about each opportunity to talk with each other. S/O react well, listen carefully, and love to see the other light up when talking. S/O express excitement with joyful reactions to each other's names, embraces, pats on the back, and handshakes. S/O's conversations are quite intense—it is not only the words that are used but also the many nonverbal gestures, eye contact, touching, hugging-there's a lot of excitement, hours can go by without making plans. S/O do not judge each other—they love to talk about anything, serious, frivolous, or just things neither would discuss with anyone else.

Discrete categories also cluster together. Affectionate encounters rely heavily on six major themes: love, care, joy, happiness, interest, excitement. Minor themes are embedder in larger narrative categories: comfort, devotion, commitment, generous, gratitude, regard, help, support, confidence, pleasure, frivolity, joking, teasing, banter, and play. Protective devices rule out calculation, manipulation, coercion, judgment, and hurt feelings. In short, a spirit of faith and fidelity in social contacts afford aesthetic explanations for working agreements that facilitate the preservation of close, intimate bonds.

It is important, however, not to leave negative displays out of the larger equation. Positive affections do not rule out negative displays but rather keeps such subversive influences under control. Likewise, negative affects do not rule out positive acts but rather relegates them to minor themes. For comparative purposes, negative disagreements can be profiled in matters of narrative priority. Sometimes what starts out as a minor point of disagreement ends up as nothing more than a single point of discord. At other times, what starts out as a single point of dispute may lead to multiple modes of dispute that resist complex resolution. Serious conflicts, nonetheless, pose important questions, puzzles, and issues that may not be easy to resolve, much less decipher. Unresolved issues or protracted disputes may be difficult to disentangle, particularly when key issues are badly conflated.

Positive affections preserve favorable conditions, meaningful engagements, and close bonds across the life span. A solid foundation of affirmative episodes may enable creative activity to expand from narrow to wider latitudes of productive outcomes. A life worth living is a life worth sharing just as well. Striving subjects can teach each other how to be fully present, overcome obstacles, magnify opportunities, and explore greater depths of shared knowledge. Moreover, a rich surplus of affirmative validations must be sufficient to reduce risk of disease and magnify health benefits. Meaningful encounters have a decisive impact on the reduction of adverse conditions and life dissatisfaction. Positive life orientations afford basic resources for robust health and well-being. Striving subjects remain extremely reliant on strong validation and unconditional confirmation from significant others. Satisfaction and meaning are closely aligned with lasting reserves of vitality, vigor, pride, joy, and zest for existence. High levels of intimacy, commitment, and responsibility all contribute to the wider search for an inspiring, productive way of life.

Signs of Disaffection

Caution is necessary. Multiple manifestations of anger, fear, and sadness to not line up in a straight line. Cause, correlation, and consequence blend together in varied pathways of intensity, salience, and persistence. Much depends on whether positive emotions displace, neutralize, or weaken harmful effects of negative reactivity. Strong anger can be displaced, without fear or sadness as side effects. Intense fear may be prolonged in compulsive-obsessive disturbances in the absence of provocative anger or lingering sadness. One category may not aggravate or dispel any other. Fear may intensify anger while sadness has the opposite effect. Likewise, rapid fear recognition may signal attention as a survival mechanism.

Threats may amplify or dampen, in ambivalent or ambiguous ways, what cannot be specified in advance. Hurt and harm are not inevitable outcomes because adaptation to anger, fear, and sadness may have protective value. Even the severity of pain depends less on internal discomfort than external hazards. Oddly, face, voice, and body language are convenient means to feign disaffections to gain tactical advantage from empathetic observers. Conversely, refusal to admit or recognize anger, fear, or sadness may be a protective or defensive means to prevent manipulative tactics from exploitive adversaries. So much depends on what types of disaffection can lead to affectionate correction. In short, there are no fixed categories for asymmetrical symptoms.

Negative affect, nonetheless, is a potent force in human encounters. We know that signs of negativity are a leading indicator of strong tendencies to discredit or devalue others in a mindless, abusive, or insensitive manner. Strong negativity, when taken personally, is painful to endure in large doses. It hurts, after all, to be repeatedly or chronically subjected to relentless or unrelieved censorship, criticism, castigation, or condemnation before other observers.

Salient signs of a negative disposition include lingering states of unhappiness, dissatisfaction, low self-esteem, mild depression, rigid, inflexible, or maladaptive styles, discredited reputation, and damaged identity. Largely implicated are signs of anger, fear, and sadness. One does not cause the other. Anger may come and go, without fear, or depression. Likewise, fear may have nothing to do with anger. Sadness may arise as cause or effect of prior disturbance. Minor episodes of disaffection are highly correlated with small talk and idle chatter.

Small Talk

S/O engage in small, talk but it soon leads to a much larger dispute—it could be anything from how to prepare potatoes to clashing views over abortion; they stay on guard because each one knows the other might devalue what is said; they don't have much respect for one another, and they never seem to think what the other is saying is right or valid. S/O talk, but S thinks O keeps things bottled up inside; usually it's the little things that add up to big things and then O withdraws until S decides to drag out the truth; O feels that little things are no big deal and shouldn't be mentioned; if it is a big enough to bug S, then S thinks it's big enough to mention, but O refuses to discuss it nonetheless. S/O never think the same thing or feel the same way; because they can't agree about anything of value, nor even how to converse in a mature fashion, brief conversations consist of small talk and nothing more; S/O get along well as long as they don't discuss any real issues; S often feels that O is looking for an argument; O will say something O knows that S does not believe; whether S ignores O or disagrees right away, O will continue to talk about it; S says things S knows will aggravate O; when O became a vegetarian, S would say things S knows would aggravate O; so S had a turkey sandwich one day and O said, "That's so disgusting, eating animal flesh" and then S made a face, smiled, finished her sandwich, and said "This tastes great." S/O used to share deep thoughts and emotions but they have grown so far apart that neither thinks intimate exchanges are appropriate nor appreciated by the other party. So they skim topics briefly, make small talk, but never truly talk anymore.

Small talk makes a virtue out of simplicity—all surface, shallow preference, no depth. Brevity is an issue when repeat offenders are construed as shortsighted when they refuse to let little things go, get caught up in minutia, devalue details, mismanage differences, quibble over semantics, display impatience, or speak without thinking. What initially appears safe and manageable territory can deteriorate quickly. There is a striking degree of mystery at work. Babble, babble, babble without end. Impatient parties indulge in small talk when they appear to be unaware of what is happening to them.

Petty arguments seem to come out of nowhere, often triggered by nothing tangible or substantial. Words and gestures cast a magic spell. Numbing, senseless banter has a certain hypnotic appeal. Minute matters can be seized and transformed into critical matters of truly mythical proportions. Baffled respondents offer no good cause or reason for what unfolds. Misery arrives in small doses that add up slowly, almost invisibly, at the periphery of working thresholds of conscious awareness and personal control. Eventually, at the little things have a larger impact that seem, upon reflection, to be badly inflated and thus culminate in a climate of resignation or acquiescence. Mutual constructions of invisible walls are real walls nonetheless to those who imagine their false imposition.

Respondents refer to minor struggles over stupid things. The issue in question may be small, a dumb little thing, something ridiculous, petty, picky, empty, pointless. Nothing substantial need be implicated. What matters most to one party may elicit a response of utter indifference to any other one. Nothing is too small or too inconspicuous to ignore. Even if the topic may qualify as stupid or trivial, those who are prone to indulge in adversarial bargains may argue anyway, even late into the night. Some profess not to be able to help themselves; others report being suckered or drawn into mindless debates over minor details. Petty bickering, slights, cuts, rips, slips, grudges, raised eyebrows or raised voices are all fair game. Nothing that registers as a meaningful act to anyone can be dismissed out of hand as meaningless gesture by anyone else. Simple events may be cut up into thin slices, one or two seconds at a time. Tedious quibbling may become the order of the day.

Trivial concerns can multiply, cluster, and congeal together into a larger, unspoken stockpile of petty complaints over minor issues that receive only indirect, tacit recognition until misrecognition of personal differences gets out of hand. The dispute in question may seem ridiculous, petty, picky, empty, or pointless. Small frictions may be construed as trivial or not worthy of dispute. However, those who indulge in adversarial bargaining may argue anyway, even late into the night. Some may profess not to be able to help themselves; others report being stuck or drawn into mindless debates about minor details. Petty bickering, slights, cuts, rips, slips, grudges, raised eyebrows, or edgy voices are all fair game. Nothing that registers as relevant to anyone can be dismissed out of hand as meaningless to anyone else who could not care less.

Simple events can be cut up into thin slices, one or two seconds at a time. Hairsplitting may become the order of the day. It is possible to become mired in clashing dualisms and sweeping imperatives. No one wants to back down or budge so much as an inch. Polarization is common when unresolved dualisms abound. Arguments are prone to argumentativeness. Often, confusion and chaos over words and gestures resembles a game without end. People spin their wheels, so to speak, but it is no avail. Fear and sadness are common outcomes when trivial matters that get out of hand.

Escalation

S/O find the more they get to know one another, it easier it is to provoke intense disputes where each one struggles to keep core beliefs intact; arguments turn into a battle for respect. S/O adapt opposite views about virtually everything; contradictions are common; S thinks O assumes everyone in the world is bad, and S sees everyone as good, until proven otherwise; O is forever the pessimist—the world will never be on his side; S is an optimist—so today was bad, tomorrow will be better; S/O have no common interest and often engage in debates just for the sake of debate. S/O don't see eye to eye on anything; what involves a simple favor to one is a sheer impossibility to the other; petty bickering is common; S/O feel so alien and they disagree about so much, talk is tedious and obnoxious; issues are dropped out of sheer frustration; so many stem from hypocrisy— O will say one thing and then do another in a vicious cycle; now S tries to avoid conversations of substance and disagreements with no solution—they just cause headaches. S/O quibble and argue all the time, mostly over semantics; they will not let minor points go, because neither one will acknowledge the other one has a point; criticism is constant; O tells S just to keep her trap shut and look pretty because men find it unattractive; S/O have such different styles that they hardly ever get along. S/O share few of the same views; daily interactions are frequent but about as deep as shot glass; they often talk about their lives together, but S disguises things because O is quick to judge what S says, and O speaks negatively about their fundamental differences which always seem to get in the way.

Discordant participants seek to control one another's thoughts and feelings but without apparent success. The law of unintended consequences is clearly at work. There is not only limited ability to shape the unfolding process but also insufficient resolve to identify alternative methods of corrective inquiry. Generally, active levels of resistance and inflexibility seem to be more powerful that what registers in the weaker and complaint forms of inaction and withdrawal into small talk and idle chatter. Moreover, there are also far more robust forms of discredit, disparagement, and devaluation at work in shared misconstructions of serious disagreement and mutual misunderstanding.

Still unanswered, however, are the causes and reasons for the persistence of misaligned activities that divisive parties know on the basis of self-reflection to cause trouble and disable shared efforts to achieve goals and fulfill purposes. In effect, many do not know why they do what they do when things go wrong, but, nonetheless, still perpetrate the same unrealistic or unobtainable outcomes. Inability and unwillingness to discuss shared faults and failures make matters worse. One thing seems certain: when one big thing goes wrong, lots of little things are sure to follow, as revealed in misaligned scripts of tension, irritation, and annoyance.

Tension

S/O talk but they are silent a lot—when they talk, it is rather tense and brief. S/O do not like each other—communication is very tense and very unnatural. S/O seem to disagree about everything, and much tension and frustration ensues. S/O used to talk but it was so tense that they don't have direct contact anymore. S/O don't see eye to eye—they end up with disagreements over any issues that might arise. S/O end up hurting one another, and this makes the apartment tense and unbearable. S/O say things just to get a rise out of each other; whenever they do see one another, each one is waiting for the other person to make some kind of move.

Irritation

S/O seem to bring out differences just to irritate one another. S/O talk, but S thinks O is irritating, and S does not know why O's presence makes S feel so on edge. S/O talk, but S thinks O says things for no apparent reason other than to irritate the hell out of S who also thinks O also says things that degrade others. S/O chose to close their system in order to avoid tension and irritation due to the fundamental differences that they cannot overcome.

Annoyance

S/O annoy the hell out of one another. S/O talk, but S finds O irritating, yet S does not know why and it's an awful feeling to feel. S/O take opposite stands on virtually everything—sometimes it gets very annoying. S/O split up, and it is so annoying to S when others tell him that they see his ex-girlfriend around and she is doing fine. S/O talked, but he wanted to be intimate and she wanted him to get lost so she found ways to reject him by getting annoyed no matter what. S/O talk, but S is insulted by the things O does; S gets annoyed with things O says, so S replies in short answers or doesn't say a lot. S/O find that talk often starts off on the wrong foot and that S gets annoyed and her anger shows (even when she tries to calm down). S/O are complete opposites; O enjoyed things that S despised and S enjoyed things that O hated—it became so annoying. S/O talk, but S thinks that O goes too far with his joking a lot and then wonders why people get annoyed at him.

Tension and annoyance are signs of weak anger. Differences outweigh similarities. Discordant parties often have no clue about what goes wrong or how to make it right. Irreconcilable differences are not readily overcome. Leading references: degradation, insult, rejection, hostility, risk of dissolution or system shutdown. Unresolved irritation and acute annoyance are ubiquitous. Mild distress is linked with hesitation and indecision as well as reluctance and discomfort.

Unspoken moods, offending manners, strong dislikes, taboo subjects, and codes of silence conspire to diminish spontaneity and synchronous talk concerning undesirable elements or unwelcome topics. The pace of speaking and listening may grind to a halt. Tense silence is awkward and typically signifies a mood of reticence and apprehension from adverse effects of so many people feelings so ill at ease, at the very same time. Unrelieved tension, irritation, and annoyance often appear to register at the periphery of conscious awareness or beyond the outer limits of personal control. Disruptive matters arouse the sort of private unpleasantness that is seldom discussed or addressed explicitly before disgruntled others.

Mild forms of unrelieved friction, strife, and strain may evolve into protracted troubles that are far more oppressive, unnatural, or even unbearable. Mounting tensions have great potential to unsettle and disable emotive stability and the larger generative process at the same time. Tension, stress, and strain resonate inside and outside of single episodes of small talk. A faulty process may give way to equally ineffective or futile ways methods of dealing with divisive topics, themes, and subjects. Hostile tactics based on button pushing or tacit provocation lead vulnerable bargainers to be on edge in what amounts to an agonistic game, a passive aggressive dual, with unspecified allowance for score keeping, pestering, teasing, joking one-up moves and subtle put-downs.

Serial discontents promote resentment, discredit, offense, insult, and crazy habits. Feelings of irritation and annoyance usually signify some measure of escalation in the sheer magnitude or salience of shared discontent or personal ill will. Though signs of displeasure of dismay may be expressed directly, underlying causes and reasons are rarely specified or appear to be remotely understood by offended parties. Mild discomfort and concealed discomfort may be elusive, puzzling, and perplexing, regardless of any sober reflection in the emotional aftermath. Serial arguments occur in ordinary exchanges over matters that prove difficult to control, though not necessarily harmful. Scaled measures of social constraint, small-scale discrepancy, dispute, and discordance all contribute to episodes of tension, irritation, annoyance, and serial argument. Relevant attributes involve chronic episodes of mutual conflict based on a spirit of discordance, disaffection, antagonism, and discontent over weak relational ties.

There is no straight line from weak anger to strong anger. Brief episodes of angry outbursts are mostly tolerable or valuable as signs of caution or something amiss. Salient indicators of more intense, salient, or protracted anger follow from a lingering spirit of discordance, disaffection, antagonism, and discontent leads to more intense, protracted trouble. Mutual divergence occurs when contending parties exhibit strong levels of misrecognized intent, misaligned perspectives, contested identity, verbal abuse, intense fighting, or problematic communication. Multiple pathways to intense anger implicate unrelieved hostility, jealousy, and hate.

Frustration

S/O talk and S will say something, but O won't acknowledge it or, worse, turn it around to mean something entirely different from what S intended; so S sits in front of O, tense and rigid, and frustration and anger are worked up until S walks away with a lot of anxiety. S/O get on each other's case; what is really detrimental is that S thinks O doesn't take anything S says seriously, or O misinterprets S's intentions—because they don't understand each other, they really have no chance to cope with disputes they may have along the way. S/O do not get along well— conversations are so surface with no meaning to them; it's so causal and boring, so S tries to act interested in what O says and does, while O seems totally uninterested in what S says and does but that's okay with S, who thinks O doesn't need to take the time to talk with S or be nice if O doesn't mean it. S/O never agree about anything—O will state O's side and S will state S's side and it begins all over again; O tells S her idea is wrong and why, and S tells O her idea is wrong and why—it's okay because it's just stupid anyway. S/O talk where controversy can go on forever without either one being able to say that one understands the other—their perspectives are from opposite ends of the spectrum, and they often cannot reach common ground.

Misrecognition of intent, divergent perspectives, and contested identity all contribute to contested frustration. Small scale conflicts, disputes, debates, and quarrels often coalesce into major differences that make a chronic difficult hard to reconcile. Inflated grievances based on divisiveness, discontent, and divergence begin to take an emotion toll on polarized advocates. Insofar as mutual identities are thrown into question, interpretive misalignments are themselves thrown into an unsettled, chaotic state. It is not so much a matter of bruised egos at stake but rather an unsettling process in which personal claims are subjected to equally personal disclaimers on the other side.

Calling into question the veracity of another person's declarations (truth claims) may also take into account any defects or deficiency in misguided presentation. Even so-called trivial disclaimers over contested subjects may convey or evoke a somber sense of displeasure with rivals to take opposing sides on decisive issues. As a result, intense wrangling about disputed matters may reflect negatively on the credibility of one who holds steadfastly to an intense issue, problem, or pressing concern. Aversive reactions are a robust predictor of frustration or acute distress. Equally distressing are shared refusals that show no willingness to lift a finger to make things better. Shared vulnerabilities to passive aggressive tactics are fully implicated in repeated frustrations that assume chronic form.

Hostility

S/O promote hostile silence punctuated by disgusted sighs. S/O talk while S thinks everything O says or does cause S to avoid O to be hostile in return. S/O talk, but ordinary conversations are hostile and heavily laden with unspoken expectations—it often has a snowballing effect, making it difficult to get out unscathed. S/O find that even civilized, small talk usually results in veiled hostility to each other.

Hostility, jealousy, and hate are murky concepts. Each one has been an intrinsic feature of misery and mayhem since the dawn of civilization. Each major category qualifies as a singular subject with wide latitudes of manifestation. Diverse variations are virtually impossible to specify with precision. Human beings produce disaffection for their own purposes. Hostility, jealousy, and hate can be justified without end.

Vindictive displays of intense disaffection must have some resilient value or else they would not be so easily justified to undermine, subvert, or invert any display of positive affections.

Desires for love, care, and affection can be turned into their extreme opposites, malice, misery, and hatred. It is virtually impossible to consign the dark side of human nature to hidden territory as it is to bring the light side to exclusive inspection. A long as supportive alignments are subject to subversive misalignment, it will not be possible to wrestle inhuman factors to the ground. There is no way for saints, heroes, and leaders to eliminate rivals, aliens, enemies from public contestation

A pragmatic model invites modest claims. Hostility, jealousy, and hate are not mere products of internal activation. None arise in a social vacuum. Discontent, disturbance, and dissonance find relief in outward projections and misattributions of unjustified accusation. Someone else or something else must serve as inflated object of false objectification. Hostility seeks revenge. Strangers, rivals, or enemies are useful scapegoats for conflated grievance or vindication. Jealousy displaces resentment, suspicion, or envy of infidelity close by (revenge) or far away (repudiation). Nothing serves self-righteous motives more than the pretense of false implications. Hate magnifies the expanse of disaffirming allegations with antipathy and intolerance of what transpires in the absolute present tense. It is difficult to displace hostility, jealousy, or hate on an external object without feeling the direct effects on an inside source.

Hostility is toxic. Extreme expressions spill over to anger, from weak to strong. Brooding, smoldering, slow-burning antagonisms blend with barely concealed bitterness or resentment. Escalating episodes of hostility, resentment, and anger may lead to unfair or unjustified misalignment when some form of responsible conduct is expected, desired, or demanded but is never forthcoming. The blind spot: it is easier to view the antagonist displays of other people to be the real (actual) source of disturbance that it is to construe one's own antipathy as the original source of self-imposed misery.

Leading narrative themes: hostile silence, lack of warmth, lots of cold responses, grudges that persist in the absence of further provocation, hostility mingled with frustration over what has gone wrong, fallen short of the mark, misdirected, or fallen apart. One can easily be exhausted: grouchy, worn out, or spent from the sheer sense of frustration and futility. It can be difficult for entrapped accusers to escape unscathed. Protracted hostility, unrelenting, unrelieved, is neither subject to moderate negotiation nor further accommodation.

Hostile persons manufacture and fabricate imagined difficulties that, long tolerated, increase vulnerability to physical illness, morbidity risks, and mortality dilution. Corrosive side effects include greater potential for defensive conflicts, misattribution, miscalculation, and withdrawal (forced retreat) into degraded mood swings that heighten susceptibility to illness, low self-esteem, and social distance. Salient markers: durable disposition to criticize, undercut, strip down, turn off, mind read, supply intentions, question motives, digress, disarm, turn off on tangents, change subject, withdraw, disengage, lapse into silence, fail to listen, observe, or care (one way or another).

Indifference and inattention, once repeated as bad habit or addiction, all to easily slides into a less meaningful way to conduct daily business. Steadfast discontent, restlessness, and irritation over trivia stand in the way: complain, vent, bitch, rant, and rail through the day and into the night. An untidy mix of uncomfortable disturbance, automaticity, and prior failures cover all that has gone wrong. Chronic aggravation is likely to generate intractable disturbance and mutual defensiveness that entrap or ensnare other observers into protracted difficulties that undermine or erode social support in a climate or atmosphere or unrelieved tension, stress, distress, mistrust, and suspicion of ulterior motives. Emotional overload only serves to make matters worse.

Jealousy

S/O are hot-blooded and loud, which makes control over emotions difficult because one always slams vicious attacks in the other's face. S thinks O is spiteful, jealous and can't handle the fact that no one wants to be like O at all. S/O fight constantly; they are opposites—S thinks O is jealous of S and O puts S down to make O feel good—O gets hostile and aggravates S on purpose, just to prey on S's weaknesses. S/o have always been so competitive—S now feels uneasy telling O things because S believes O is jealous of S's ex-boyfriend, because O has spent so much time cutting S and her ex-boyfriend down.

Jealousy makes control over intense or complex emotions more difficult. Spite, bitterness, resentment, irritation, and aggravation combine to reveal personal weaknesses, shortcomings, vulnerabilities, faults, and failures in feeble or futile engagements at restorative modes of sensemaking activity. As a result, people feel on edge, indignant, provocative, or vicious in matters of character assassination and personal attacks where respective parties constantly strive to edge each other out.

Jealous sentiments in romantic relations surface in responses to external competition and exclusionary personal boundaries as sources of great apprehension and uncertainty with great potential for hurt and harm as major transgressions. Jealousy often results in intense surveillance behavior, such as spying, checking up, keeping track, looking for telltale signs of trouble, and self-indulgence in clinging or desperate maneuvers under covert operations, even if at great expense to one's own sense of dignity, worth, and self-regard. Jealous feelings in loving relations are related negatively to member satisfaction. Sexual jealousy acquires social definition in each highly charged atmosphere.

Jealousy may merge with evocative features of anger, fear, and sadness. It is not clear whether chronic disagreement fosters jealousy, whether jealousy is disagreeable, or whether unspecified blends of mounting negativity comes with a sense of impending loss of someone or something that matters a great deal. Moreover, jealous attributions may be accusatory or confessional. An admission of jealousy is neither self-enhancing or self-compensatory but rather an ugly admission or confession of a socially undesirable trait on the surface but pervasive underneath. Personal disclaimers abound, of course, precisely because they are so effortless and easy to produce. Furthermore, the jealous party may be demonized as frivolous, mindless, dismissive, impatient, interruptive or guilty of greater crimes—mainly variations of personal attack. Flirtatious behavior is innocent and a useful way to break the ice among previously unacquainted persons. However, often what starts out as harmless or benign translates into heavy score keeping on all sides.

Ambiguity and confusion are evident in the all-purpose fact that virtually anyone or anything can serve as a signal or sign of something deeper at stake. Petty resentment, argument, bickering, or episodic fights may offer sufficient justification for mutual silence or lateral refusal to acknowledge jealous sentiments over what grants credit to someone at the expense of someone else's loss. Possibilities are endless. Occasions for jealous crosscurrents are imagined without end. Steadfast inability to confront such disturbing or disquieting possibilities of sexual, aesthetic, or ethical violations may leave some beleaguered partners frozen or suspended, as in a state of paralysis over terrible secrets or unspoken lies.

Hate

S/O talk, but now S hates O and avoids contact as much as possible. S/O broke up because S could not stand anyone on Earth worse than his ex-girlfriend, and S can't believe he wasted six months of his life with this schizophrenic, dual-personality, chemically imbalanced, possessive, domineering, bitch; S can honestly say he wishes she did not exist. S/O try to talk, but S hates to begin to talk to O about anything because of the fact that they disagree about everything. S/O usually only interact in the morning and at night, so it is very causal surface information, boring, with no meaning at all; S thinks that O is very funny and lively but O makes a lot of negative comments; "I hate it when…" or "it bugs me that…'; it gets hard to hear over and over. S/O talk, but S thinks that she is always sees herself as being right and can't be wrong, even if she is completely wrong; S hates it when O does ridiculous things, and he doesn't mind telling her at all—O hates the fact that S always disagrees with her so forcefully, but S always tells his other friends what S is thinking without holding back. S/O talk in ways that make O thinks S likes O, but S doesn't really like O and S hates it when men think she likes them when she doesn't like them at all.

Hate is a heavy burden. It is difficult to hate another person without feeling hate for oneself. Intense hate cannot be projected outward without seeping inward. The wish to harm others is painful to accuser and accused alike. Hatred blurs the lines between source and object, intention and effect. Unbridled hatred, in other words, is transactive. It migrates rather than settles at a point of origin or destination. If hatred arises from devalued weakness, strength emerges from valued ties with significant others. Hate thrives on repudiation of life affirming valuations. In metaphoric terms, hate is a brutal choice of death over life. Life is no longer worth living when death is allowed to take its place. Suicide and murder are not easily dispelled. Signs of disgust and contempt figure heavily in social reproduction of violence, malice, and bitter hatred.

Contempt, shame, and humiliation seem to go hand in hand. Poor impulse control and unthinking revulsion promote the durability of disgust over aberrant sensibilities. It is a sad truth that some chronically miserable people stay in hateful relations for inexplicable reasons, regardless of the magnitude of hidden damage or eventual costs. Reciprocated hatred can take a tremendous toll on body, mind, and spirit. Death wishes can be pushed beyond the outer limits of tolerance. A living hell does not require belief in hell after life. Intimate relations may be pressed to a radical court of last resort. Total aversion to intimacy may entail a stance of malignant vindictiveness, whereby severe strife is acquired, manufactured, and fabricated from relentless and steadfast insistence on pressing one lethal claim against another, tit-for-tat, without let-up, break, or relief in sight.

A vicious cycle may emerge from persistent application of radical aggressive or defensive measures that leave wounded victims alienated yet idealized at the same time. Human relations illuminate character traits that in turn are subject to sharp focus and specificity of demands, commands, injunctions, instructions, declarations, and categorical imperatives. What hurts, from a relational perspective, is the sheer magnitude of discrepancy between idealized image and concrete reality. When each partner seeks frantically to fulfill idealized aspects of personal identity, rigid conditions are set up where the needs of each of the members are bound to fail. Rage, spit, and vindictiveness are not all that difficult to dredge up where friend and lover transform themselves into foe and enemy.

Fear

S/O talk, but conversations all end up on an unhappy note, regardless of the cause of faulty communication; S tries to avoid O out of fear of another unpleasant episode. S/O talk, but S can't express herself freely—she fears rejection and therefore doesn't express herself enough. S/O clash in ways that make S think that O has fear of things that don't mesh well with is scheme of life. S/O discuss touchy issues where both are irrational; instead of trying to grasp each other's view, they degrade one another's views; part of these reactions stem from fear, and others from feelings of rage and mistrust. S/O argue, and O defends her ideals and feels the need to attack S's thoughts and feelings; S tries not to react to O's arguments, fearing her wrath and seeing no point in a fight; O, on the other hand, seem to thrive on provoking fear and opposing S at all costs.

What is so striking is how fearful rivals may weaken strong ties and strengthen weak ties. The stronger the scale, scope, or salience of discord, the more that fear and apprehension are likely to be about complex matters of closeness and intimacy. Profound discords have considerable potential for opposing parties to distance themselves both linguistically (from opposite stands on issues) emotionally, aesthetically, and spiritually (from each other).

Unspoken, invisible, and intangible forces and factors may inhibit, restrict, or preclude sensitive issues from coming to the surface of mutual observation. Social reproduction of mutual fear registers in the urge, striving, or aspiration to move away, change focus, redirect energy, withdraw, escape, or explore alternative options. Thematically, a spirit of trepidation, fear, and loathing culminates in a greater measure of denial access (e. g., modes of escapism, xenophobia, indifference, alienation, malaise, shyness, emptiness, or isolation), missed opportunities for future interaction (e.g., missing out, failing, and disconnection), and bitter retreat into vicarious or imaginary modes of lies, illusions (e.g., secrets, dreams, fantasies, illusions, withdrawal into fictious worlds).

A toxic climate of fear pervades troubling or disturbing human encounters in which signs of danger and risk are central features of narrative themes. What adds insult to injury are strong signs of disrespect too significant and decisive to ignore as symbolic markers of injury, hurt, and harm perpetrated on unwilling or unwelcome subjects. Hence, primordial fear and trepidation are magnified by the sheer strength of aversive devaluation and degradations. Extreme fear by be inexpressible for the very fear of its effect.

Sadness

S/O talk while O performs "funny" little things on people she may not even know and makes them feel humiliated and worthless; personally, this makes S feels this to be obnoxious, mean, degrading, and sad. S/O have face-to-face contract that is almost always a disaster; conversations are always brief and tense; S dislikes arguments with O, so S thinks how sad it is they have become so indifferent and that they cannot tolerate each other's presence. S/O do not see eye to eye; they do not feel comfortable sharing personal things, and it is all very sad and very odd to S. SO endure a sad situation; they are not soul sisters but rather eternal adversaries. S/o have mostly one-way talks; it is sad that O is a nice person and means well but she does not understand that she talks too much.

Failure is instructive, however, if only in hindsight. Mutual sadness involves broken dreams, lost hope, lack of desire, or unfilled promises. Bitterness is a reminder of all that has been lost, misplaced, discarded, abandoned, or forsaken. Sober reflection often entails "what if" or "if only" counterfactual projections of shared episodes that miss the mark or fall short of the mark. Expectancy violations maybe far and few between, or they may acquire a density, a thick mass of momentum, as in a cloud of doom. Unspoken assumptions of further entrapment in future resignation are tacit promises to perpetuate trials and tribulations as a daily routine, a constant burden, as falling into an aimless or lost way of shared life.

Adverse outcomes promote a residue of guilt, shame but most sad parties reveal little concern, regret, or remorse about things that turn out badly for other people in their midst. Resignation is a common response to protracted sadness or lingering depression. Passivity is a key source of negative affect that amplifies adverse outcomes of boundary crossing, trespass, offense, and moral failure. So striking is the sheer passivity of those who subject other people to all manner of ill will, unprovoked discontent, and then, after the fact, leave out a critical factor—regret. False innocence covers a multiplicity of small sins and slippery misdemeanors.

A larger implication is worthy of mention. Topics of affirmation may be inspected separately as discrete categories. In the messy reality of daily life, however, affirmative activities are always at risk from subversive influences. Good stuff and bad stuff reside side-by-side, for better or for worse, more of one, less of the other. Boundary lines and boundary violations are integrated into larger spheres of social alignment. There is, therefore, a distinction to consider. Amicable subjects are more able to nurture, expand, and preserve a strong, abiding surplus of positive thoughts and feelings.

When affirmative subjects to encounter brief episodes of dispute, conflict, argument, working disagreement, or mutual misunderstanding, they are in a better position to take corrective action, return back, through restorative devices, to recalibrate the wide expanse of multiple expressions of positive affect, sympathy, and regard. Conversely, when disaffected subjects allow a surplus of brief episodes of dispute, conflict, argument, working disagreement, or mutual misunderstanding to be neutralized in mixed outcomes, they are more likely to slide back (regressively) in negative displays of disaffection. Thereby, positive gains are dislocated, while negative losses take their place. Once valued resources are allowed to dissipate, it is unlikely that broken pieces will be put back together again.

Summary

So far, a life worth living has been charted across three broad venues of stable meaning systems. Inspiration stems from recognition of one's rare, unique, and distinctive place in the larger scheme of things. The universe is the ultimate source of material and energy that registers in physical force and social influence, vigor and vitality, across multiple spheres of success and failure in goal-directed aims. Favorable conditions of mortal existence require a safe and secure site of habitation, strong genes, general intelligence, and altruistic kinship ties. A robust system of affirmative activities relies on core values, tolerance of fallible achievements, positive episodes of based on a rich surplus of live, care, joy, happiness, interest, and excitement. However, subversive signs of disaffection must also be taken into strategic account. Trivial matters have an uncanny way of migrating into escalated tensions, irritation, annoyance, hostility, jealousy, and hate. Anger, fear, and sadness are signs of decay, deterioration, and degradation, in quality of life and longevity expectations. Social cohesion adds what subversive influences subtract. Civilization requires access to repair and restoration of humane interventions to assure distributive justice and a brighter future for future generations.

4

Collective Knowledge

A life worth living requires social knowledge and cultural intelligence. Intelligence specifies. Culture generalizes. One sphere does not transfer to the other. IQ tests are individually scored, socially acquired, and culturally applied. Nothing is fixed or rigidly imposed along the way. Critical distinctions between worth or lack of worth, relevant or irrelevant, useful or useless, are not effortlessly disentangled. It takes a great deal of labor-intensive effort to figure out what to include or exclude from daily projects. Likewise, a wide expanse of open space is required to navigate across a familiar domain or a foreign territory.

Survival mandates constant adaptation to shifting contours of globalization, technology, infrastructure, demography, literature, and social mobility. Fortunately, staggering transformations of human knowledge, dispersed through media, are accessible to a larger proportion of world population. Boundaries between large-scale systems (democratic deliberations) and small-scale systems (communication networks) are now more fully integrated than ever before. Conversely, lingering pockets of unjustified ignorance defy explanation.

Disinformation takes a tremendous toll. Make no mistake. Metaphors can be misleading. Neither the acquisition of social knowledge or cultural intelligence are universally valued or inexorably pursued. Sometimes it may be prudent to settle for just enough of a stable baseline of fact and interpretation to get by, from one day to the next. Infinite expanse of personal knowledge or cultural sensitivity is neither feasible nor plausible. Cheerful invocations to 'quest' or 'growth' models are notoriously one-sided. It may appear convenient to exaggerate provision for human desire than to admit what is necessary for reasonable decision-making or emotional security in daily life.

Appeal to a 'socially desirability' bias may ignore or minimize 'socially undesirable' features of information detection. Conflated inscriptions of 'more' or 'better' pathways to wise counsel do not yield to 'upward' or 'forward' progress, without allowance for 'downward' or 'backward' modes of regressive outcomes. What nature opens up spring and summer it closes down fall and winter. Similarly, life gains in youth what it loses with age.

A pragmatic model is better able to trace uneven contours across the life span. There must be open provision for dual options: inclusion and exclusion, expansion and contraction, progression and regression. Unspecified allowance for productive gains gives way to unproductive loss. What mortal existence affords may be taken away. No wonder information can be construed as a threat. Authoritarian, dictatorial regimes are implacable enemies of free speech, assembly, and civil liberties. Repressive rhetoric relies on subterfuge, subversion, and suppression to replace inconvenient truths with convenient lies.

Goal-directed Aims

Human beings protect meaning systems as a way to define a unique position and place in the wider world. The tension between distinct identity and shared construction is not easily resolved. The search for indelible meanings implies broad tolerance for integrated outcomes. There is no escape from total immersion within the wider province of the ecological landscape. Meaning is intrinsic to the transfer of scarce resources from one person or group to another. Multiple human contacts fortify goal-driven enactments of prevailing cultural rituals, routines, and symbolic artifacts. Diverse linguistic traditions rive rise to material affordances of collective appropriation. Observation and participation give way to working agreement and mutual understanding of what is essential for realistic appraisal.

Knowledge systems underscore the need for logical and reasonable responses to diverse conflicts and contested viewpoints in the public sphere. Striving subjects need not aspire to goals derived from a maximization principle—as a drive or urge to achieve the highest possible good. Moderation favors informed desire, compromise, and consensus over what levels of pleasure, freedom, autonomy, and independence are available.

Neither imitation or inspiration need to be judged by rare or exceptional achievers. After all, there are immense pressures that must be tolerated for singular achievements of gifted experts. Socially valuable knowledge requires credibility and currency in personal, relational, ethnic, and cultural negotiations. What matters to effective daily functioning is the requisite ability to accurately characterize other subjects and to use observed inferences as a means to secure feasible goal-directed aims.

Some goals are enacted in simple, automatic routines. Other are stored in selective attention. Whereas lived experience shapes short-term meaning as attributed to situational cues, long-term goals are more directed to the salience of environmental awareness. Acquired meanings are filtered through the lens of preparation and practice for the acquisition of improved performance. Knowledge construction expands from concerns about what others think and do along with equal consideration about the usefulness, adequacy, and improvability of new ideas. Shared knowledge extends beyond small-scale systems to wider parameters of large-scale organizations, institutions, and network collaborations. Goal selection and valued priorities align with compensation to counteract loss of meanings that are no longer secure.

Linguistic Inheritance

Cultural evolution is goal directed. Human aspirations are constructed out of the real-world conditions that surround them. The use of complex language enables human beings to transform the cultural inheritance and fulfill basic tasks associated with the need for individual security and collective well-being. Tension, strife, and strain are decisive factors in shaping the potential for violence, peace, or conflict to be altered or changed in social and cultural organization. At issue is the dynamic interplay between violent acts and the linguistic atmosphere that surrounds them. In effect, the routine misuse or abuse of language contributes to the question of how well or badly human beings treat one another on a larger scale.

Conditions of violence, peace, and conflict are manifest as distinctive achievements and as abstract objectives of universal aims. One implication is clear. If we want to make the world a better place, we must be prepared to 'construct' less violent means of cohabitation and communication. A central task is to trace shared effort and collective movement away from radical disaffections implicit in acts of physical violence and toward their most plausible symbolic counterparts.

On a small scale, human encounters have unintended consequences and social implications. On a larger scale, humans, unlike other animals, have well-developed capacities and abilities to transmit information, not just laterally, within generations, but vertically across generations. Intergenerational conflict is widespread and pervasive throughout the animal kingdom. Human conflict, it turns out, is simply the most complicated, obdurate, and potentially liberating source of conflict in the entire ecosystem. What stands out about so much small-scale human conflict is the sheer magnitude of what is possible.

Struggle and strife permeate human interactions in distinctive ways that are quite peculiar to the species. It is apparent, therefore, that human beings are fully capable of anticipating, maintaining, and resolving a wider range of conflicts than is any other species on the Earth. In terms of the sheer magnitude of what is possible, human beings have an enormous competitive edge that gathers momentum over time. Evolution, after all, is a process in time in which possibility and potentiality are important factors in establishing the conditions necessary for future elaboration. What acquires momentum are the unique effects and outcomes that make the greatest difference as a consequence of their total individual and collective use.

Ironically, the notion of humans having a 'competitive edge' over the linguistic capacity of other species may well ignore a primordial problem that all humans share. We have the power to preserve or destroy one another, and other living creatures. The enormous power of language, historically speaking, is quite a recent arrival on the human scene. Such a sweeping capacity to solve problems on a global scale cannot be separated from an equally greater potential to wreak havoc and reproduce some of the most horrendous problems on the Earth. Against the global backdrop of threat and insecurity, the power of ordinary language can be seen as both curse and cure. By extension, life affirming meaning systems are a critical source of protection and defense against violent erosions that are everywhere to be found.

Questions of sustenance, security, and well-being go together, after all, because the human world is a material world and human beings are physical beings who have devised complex modes of language use, in some measure, as expressive mechanisms to facilitate individual reproduction and to enhance the perpetuation of the human race. As a consequence, public conflicts may be viewed as linguistic struggle and strife over the distribution of scarce resources—material, economic, and symbolic—in the human world. Personal conflicts are designed to facilitate the redistribution whatever it is that humans lack but nonetheless value. From a global standpoint, human knowledge is transmitted through local and regional languages that remain obscure or incomprehensible to proximate neighbors or across cultural boundaries. Historical, regional, local, contextual, and situational are significant, therefore, in shaping the selective and strategic nature of speaking environments.

Shared activities are observed for the effects they produce on others and are repeated thereafter for the sake of those effects. By these standards, human interactions are sustained in a global network of real-testing ceremonies where elaborated forms of language use are subject to an uneven mix of 'facilitative' and 'subversive' influences. Single acts of observation are taken to be intrinsic aspects of the definition of the total situation.

Individual activities are subject to a wide range of (re) interpretation from a constantly changing or shifting array of reference points. The question of 'what' gets presented by one party is relative to 'how' it is to be represented by any other. In effect, language and culture act as twin filters to regulate and monitor various conceptions of individuality, separation, and the degree of relatedness of individuals to each other.

Complex language gives prior and implicit conditions an explicit form of mutual expression. Matters of definition, classification, and explanation involve a dynamic process where each expressive act is embedded within a larger sequence that may establish new possibilities for further explication. Evolutionary change promotes the use of activities outside the body for functions previously performed by the body itself. The larger process favors gradual transformation of individually sustained activities into those shared with many others. In critical situations the selection of those who speak is largely at the expense of non-speakers. What matters is not simply the long-term survival of the most articulate but the slow disappearance of the most inarticulate members of society. Moreover, those who speak well acquire or derive a host of secondary advantages over those who speak less well. At stake is the total magnitude of what is lost or gained at each step along the way.

Complex Language

Skillful use of complex language is highly advantageous. Differential sensitivity to slight variations in ordinary language use constitutes a basic human resource in matters to facilitate (1) constructive thinking; (2) adaptation to changing, unforeseen, adverse, or unwelcome circumstances; (3) cognitive growth; (4) resilient meaning; (5) quality of life; and (6) the odds of survival. Conversely, systematic misuse, abuse, or neglect of something at once so powerful and mysterious can be quite hazardous to one's health and well-being.

Complex language allows the highly skilled to sustain daily interactions in ways that affect considerations of individual integrity in the short-run and collective survival in the long-run. This is the case not only for matters of nourishment and sustenance but also for those affecting questions of social status and mate selection, two major determinants of the ability of a speaker to reproduce at regional and collective levels of existence.

The wider the latitude of linguistic conditions that individuals are able to bring under a greater measure of control, the more each party is placed in an enhanced position to maintain close and enduring ties with other people. When dealing with other people, not material objects, skilled speakers call upon the richest expressive and responsive resources. In matters involving personal cooperation, negotiation, manipulation, and scheming to get our own way, subtle and intricate aspects of language use are quite involving and highly salient. When disputes grow dangerous, language is needed as an alternative to violent forms of retribution and reprisal. Language is both a 'collective' resource to enrich the quality of life and a widely acknowledged 'personal' resource to facilitate renewed relations and vastly more complex organization of human society. By implication, anything that can be a resource for one person may be viewed a liability by any other.

The potential for language use to prevail violent actions is largely mediated through the preservation and cultivation of life-affirming rituals. In this equation, humans realize the greater potential for physical violence to erupt and strive, therefore, to civilize, appease, or tame the larger destructive threat through the daily (re)invocation of a litany of life-affirming customs, practices, and projects.

Rituals of conversation, in particular, provide a margin of open-ended and low-risk opportunity to reveal or explore a rapid succession of aggressive urges and affectionate needs simultaneously. In this way, evolutionary change slowly expands the human capacity to love or hate, like or dislike, in relation to who is identified as friend or foe or seen as close by or far away.

Under favorable conditions, the threat of murder and sacrifice may be slowly displaced or deflected by collective participation in shared actions designed to transform high-risk violent urges into low-risk symbolic substitutes. In this way, refined use of language and communication is able to take some of the sting out of the potential for sudden outbreaks of violence. Conversely, daily rituals, projects, and routines may reverse, sometimes in a regressive way, the slant or tone of the larger enterprise. The misuse and abuse of abstract concepts, for example, may transgress and violate human sensibilities to the point of great injury and harm.

The question of what makes life worth living is not sealed up in lofty aspirations. Instead, a worthy life must be reality-tested against all of the risks, dangers, and hazards that stand to undermine odds of survival. Conditions of violence, peace, and conflict are linguistically constructed. Language is power. A wide array of facilitative and subversive influences are intrinsic factors in reality construction. It is a mistake, therefore, to reduce signals, signs, and symbols to incidental aspects of style, fades, or fashion. Without sufficient provision for the vitality of meaning systems, human beings are far less able to control their own destiny.

Sense-Making Practice

Human beings are sensitive to the question of what transpires when things go well or turn out badly. Each individual has deeply ingrained cognitive mechanisms to identify and categorize what sorts of things fit well together and what types do not. A succession of high-order achievements facilitates a greater measure of appreciation of the distinctive value of what takes place. Favorable conditions are known to confer a broad range of secondary benefits. These include, among other things, personal sensitivity to the expenditure of scarce recourse, willingness to contribute good ideas, faith in the pursuit of personal goals as worth the cost, and especially enhanced communicative skills.

By these standards, unfavorable conditions include any harsh, unsafe, degraded, unhealthy, or otherwise unsuitable environments for human language to multiply and flourish. Discursive practices, after all, do not spring out of thin air. A rich confluence of behavioral and environmental factors must surely come together to secure a state of harmony and accord for all who are concerned.

Diminished resolve to tolerate dispute or discord may weaken the wider search for common ground. Moreover, severe distortions in thought and feeling may become deeply ingrained in protracted episodes of badly misinterpreted or misaligned forms of social action. An upsurge of unwanted internal interference and external distraction add further to the overall level of bias, static, and noise in the larger system.

Favorable conditions are shown to benefit core matters affecting the critical evaluation of personal performance in various public contexts. The distinction between 'effective' and 'faulty' interaction is quite decisive. An effective way of life is associated with the all-inclusive ability to adapt to changing or unforeseen circumstance. Matters of efficacy in self-expression require the ability to construct reasonably clear definitions of what transpires and an inclusive sense of direction from one moment to the next. In sharp contrast are those shared actions with unclear definition (aimlessness, lack of focus) or direction (indecision). In comparative terms, a refined sense of personal clarity is useful in maintaining close ties with others. Likewise, the absence of these same qualities is conducive to the formation of weaker ties with others.

Faulty or ineffective actions imply a marked discrepancy between an individual's capacity or self-expression and subsequent evaluations of the performance in question by observers. A poor quality or low-level performance may be taken as weak, inarticulate, misaligned, or misapplied by one observer or another. In contrast, a good or efficacious performance may be viewed as strong, explicit, articulate, well aligned, or closely in synch (by some standard). At issue is what diverse types of personal conduct are to be construed by others as well functioning, whole, and integrated, or else dismissed as fragmented, divided, and split.

Practical logic is indispensable for sense-making practice. Solid reasons connect factual evidence to credible claims. Strong claims qualify as objective only if certified in valid form. Progression from warrant to conclusion takes place in such a way as to unite explicit observation with diverse inferences and tacit implications in a coherent, goal-directed manner. Reasonable standards help to make sense of things by arranging a set of particulars into a larger cluster of progressive movements.

Personal logic can be employed to support and nurture, or subvert and undermine, the vitality of a reasonable process. Logical appeals serve useful purposes. Explicit reasons clarify thoughts, feelings, and actions. Knowing what seems logical to someone else makes it easier to address serious topics from multiple viewpoints. There may be some gain or pleasure in being in touch with alternative ways that others use to make sense of things. It is better to reason out things together than to go it all alone.

The case for constructive argument is derived from the generative capacity or ordinary language itself. Salient topics qualify as being at once innovative, infinite, and inexhaustible. When effectively applied by strong advocates who are both competent and credible, reason in controversy produces generative themes linked with informed logic and supporting material in endless variety.

Constructive arguments provide an effective means to improve the strength of relational ties by keeping viable disputes alive. The likelihood of achieving positive outcomes depends largely on whether articulate advocates are in a favorable position to test each other's ideas rather than test their personal deficiencies.

Congenial requirements include a requisite base of resources, abilities, and skills sufficient to treat other advocates as equals, fine common ground, move away from extreme claims in favor or moderation, exploit attitudinal similarities in each other's evolved perspectives and worldly outlooks. Constructive advocates foster congenial outcomes that are usually missing from fare more competitive or aggressive confrontations.

Whatever is subject to the unified force of reasoning well together is, by definition, also subject to the countervailing influence of illogical, unreasonable, or senseless response to collective involvement in viable modes of societal constructions. In effect, the best of intentions cannot provide surefire protection or firm assurance against unwelcome imposition of unreasonable or careless reliance on weak warrants for unjustified conclusions based on false assumptions. The ultimate rationale of 'all speaking well' is subject to all manner of compromised convictions and expedient alternatives that are misguided features of everyday life.

Those who are highly skilled in applying exacting standards of applied logic cannot be so isolated from the presence of others who employ inexact and imprecise logic in the midst of inflated contentions. A goal of reaching consensus, based on convincing arguments, does not mean the unity of reason will prevail over the disunity of fragmented reason.

Protracted conflicts over irreconcilable differences proliferate so massively that irrational ranting may leave no room for sensible appeals to prevail. Shrill reliance on emotional overload tends to mask, confuse, or disguise deeper intractable for which logical appeals and factual claims do not lend themselves to common access to realistic standards of informed judgment.

When obscurity rules, the best arguments are not to be found. Wishing does not make it so. What qualifies as irrational behavior is, in fact, virtually anything or everything that may go astray or turn out wrong. What is construed by one advocate as being senseless may range in scale from sheer trivia to a supreme test of ultimate conviction. When irrational advocates do not have their way, they are prone to displace hostility and anger on to other people. Even worse, they are not apt to think clearly about what they are doing before they are doing it; or they get so caught up in intense struggle over aversive emotional states that they lose touch with varied appeals to common sense.

Where there is no room for the corrective, persuasive power of reasoned discourse, there can be no way to express or respond to risk or threat. Sometimes, unreasonable, illogical advocates of argumentative claims may discover they are addressing an audience of one. Common maladies include argument for arguments sake; stubbornness; closed mindedness; right fighters (who's right/ who's wrong) and score keeping.

Contrasts are striking. Agreeable logic is constructive. Affirmative references describe skill in argument as being sufficient, compelling, and well-matched: S/O argue from assertive positions; at the end, there are no clear answers but two well-argued sides. S/O know each other so well that when they do argue, they soon realize each other's points, so dispute does not last long. S/O hardly ever argue; when they do, they make up rather quickly because they cannot go without the other person for very long. S/O love to argue—they pick each other's brains to get at the heart of the matter. S/O agree about most things on a general scale, but they both love to argue small details just for the sake of arguing and the competition it generates. S/O do not argue over issues—they just listen to the other's opinion and find out why the other feels the way the other does. S/O rarely argue because they both know how the other is going to react in any situation. S/O find on the surface that they mock, argue, and disagree constantly, but on a higher level they know it is okay to hold different viewpoints and still understand each other/ S/O can count on one hand the number of times that they have argued over the past two years of friendship—if they do argue at all, it only takes a few minutes to work things out. S/O rarely argue because they both are fear the loss of each other.

Disagreeable logic is a waste of time. S/O disagree with each other on so many issues that they can hardly argue anymore—it seems useless. S/O begin to argue more and more about less and less. S/O always fight about something—it must be some type of competition, but it seems they will still argue about trivial things. S/O continue to argue because it pisses them off and everyone else too. S/O end up arguing about something they should not discuss anyway—their only agreement is to stop talking about sensitive things that they will just argue about anyway. S/O argue—then O stares off in silence, S looks around, then smiling at the stupidity of the argument, shakes her head; when they disagree, O faces away from S (in despair) and S will shake her head in disgust until she decides to end the argument. S/O argue all the time about everyday issues; S often finds himself arguing against O just to prove him wrong. S/O argue because they do not have any patience anymore. S/O argue often about differences of opinion. S may see it one way and O may see it another, yet they do not really care one way or another about the disputed issue in question. S/O talk, but S thinks it is pointless to argue because O believes he is the center of the universe and the only things in life are hockey and women. S/O) frequently argue about the little things. S/O argue with each other, become hostile, and accomplish nothing. S/O find there are not many situations in which they do not argue. S/O will not let minor details go because neither one wants to acknowledge that the other has a point. S/O don't argue all that much, but when they do, nothing really seems to get resolved. S/O both feel they have all the correct answers, so when either one tries to make a comment, they always contradict each other and argue each other's points.

The central finding is striking. Arguments are not usually frequent, conspicuous, prolonged in affectionate relations where a climate of working agreement and mutual understanding prevail. Conversely, arguments are frequent, troublesome, problematic, and destructive of personal relations where working disagreement and mutual misunderstanding prevail. The full magnitude of difference occurs at two broad levels of explanation. High levels of competence and compatibility are likely to sustain reason controversy. Lower levels of competence and compatibility are likely to typify retrograde qualities of unreasonable disputes. In effect, a working base of working agreement and mutual understanding overlap with conditions that are associated with aspirations toward excellence in matters of argument and advocacy.

Resolvability of personal differences is a major theme. Dispute does not last long. Explore issues. Wind up justifying each other's ideas. Reach compromise that does not belittle anyone. Stay flexible, trust, enjoy talk, get things through, make up quickly, make sure each one's ideas and believes are clear to everyone else. Conversely, potential resolution is diminished for those who argue frequently without solutions; rarely settle disputes because neither party want to be wrong or admit the other might be right; decide it is not worth the time or energy; argue about nothing and leave with discontent. Wish it had never begun; become sick of seeing each other; refuse to speak for days, weeks, or months.

Miscommunication

What makes life worth living does not require flawless communication. There is growing recognition that language use, communicative practices, is pervasively, intrinsically flawed, partial, and problematic. In human affairs, no one is infallible. The margin of difference between success and failure is a matter of 'more or less' rather than 'all or nothing.' In the moment-by-moment sequences of transfer and translation, it is virtually impossible to discuss subject matter with anyone who has not previously been aware of the existence of that subject (qua subject). Since the rules of conventional language use are not identical from one speaker to another, each language has a unique potential for reality construction—each subtends a different set of potential realities.

It is important, therefore, not to impose impossible standards on realistic standards of collective knowledge or cultural intelligence. The search for a good life need not aspire to achieve an idealist state of purified exaltation. It is a relief to know that nullities—weakness, limitation, and vulnerability—are part of the cosmic bargain. Therefore, it is not necessary to chase after utopian desires. What matters is direct access to a standard of sufficient dedication to a higher cause than what unbridled self-interest can afford.

Skilled speakers are best prepared to engage in acts of mutual influence where the ground rules of situated knowledge are clearly specified or well known in advance. Routine interactions take place insofar as the parties in question are able to rely on a stable tradition of prior contacts for tacit guidance and direction in deciding what to do now or next. However, when dealing with unusual or uncertain circumstance, there may be greater difficulty in coping with rapidly increased levels of complexity, complication, and loss of control (long-term). Specific problems may pile up, one after another, without an equal number of solutions in sight. Where complete communication (total influence) is ruled out, partial communication (miscommunication) may still be construed as worthy of (incomplete) success. Sometimes it is better to tolerate what can be achieved (we did our best) than to focus on incomplete or unsettled business.

Problematic encounters produce complicated or unsettled questions that may exceed the higher thresholds of competence and compatibility that are available at the time. A problematic issue registers as an arch riding concern that does not lend itself to any apparent or self-evident means of articulation, course of action, or mode of resolution. Sometimes the world is too much with us. Personal burdens may be too much to bear. Striving subjects are vulnerable to 'impossible' situations (double binds) where nothing can make things better or keep them from getting worse. The specific value of a problematic issue corresponds roughly with the total magnitude of what is at issue or construed as outstanding, unresolved, unsettled, or unknow.

It is not always possible to know what to do to find a way out of a jam. It is, in other words, a matter of the collective capacity to attend to the accumulation of unfinished business. At no point is there any assurance that (complete) communication will be certain or relatively trouble free. By comparison, critical or urgent situations can be quite vexing to figure out when they operate at the outer limits of volition and conscious awareness.

Problem-solutions models suffer from recognition that not all messy problems are amenable to tidy solutions. If resolute subjects could resolve all of their intolerable problems, there would be nothing left to do. Invasive actions, natural disasters, serious illness, death of family members, threaten prior beliefs, and entrenched behavioral maladies. In addition, severe trauma causes people to reconstruct belief systems and design alternative explanations for life-altering events that are not easy to comprehend, much less explain to anyone else.

Human encounters are fascinating and elusive. So many things take place at once, all the time. Each source contributes to the definition and direction of a shared situation and yet the totality of mutual influence goes well beyond the grasp of any one member. In symbolic interaction, no one is located in an ideal, optimum, or privileged position to keep track of what that takes place for the very same reasons there are no independent or infallible standards of determination. Because attention is selective, lots of stuff takes place beyond our slanted grasp.

In matters of what separates this from that, more or less, better or worse, each participant has an unspecified margin of opportunity to make a difference in what transpires. Yet, at all points along the way, all that is manifest is based on a slant, angle, and view of the larger scheme of things. In other words, each observer expresses more than what any other can grasp or comprehend. In effect, each party provides an alternative account for what takes place collectively. Lived experience insures there are no exact replications or duplications, unlike computer calculations, robotic repetition, or internet copies.

Social interactions produce a rich mix of implicit urges, desires, intentions, expressions, lines of action, functions, effects, and outcomes. Distinctive features congeal into a holistic and synthetic rubric that does not reduce itself to simple verdicts over whether message sent equals message received. Sign making efforts differ in clarity, ranging anywhere from utter transparency to the totally opaque. Signals of disclosure and concealment are located on all sides. Such an abstract concept rules out the possibility of self-evident modes of transfer, translation, or interpretation. In active reference to the linguistic construction of reality, it is necessary to incorporate aspects of miscommunication. What defies description are critical thresholds of plurality—what each striving subject feels, thinks, or attempts to say or do. Inexplicable conditions are acute when multiple participants confront unusual, confusing, or novel sensibilities that prove difficult to specify to anyone else on the strength of words and gestures alone.

What defies description are complex, multifaceted and innovative aspects of sensory activation that a given source has never dealt with before. It can be difficult to define what is felt in a concise or clear manner. There may be times when there are no words or gestures in anyone's lexicon to express exactly what is ascribed at the time. Unconscious sensations jumble into a knot. One may not untangle the jumble until complex factors are worked out in one's restless mind; and only then might it be possible to identify, dissect, pull apart, put together and finally identify distinct features and uncertain ambiguities.

What one experiences in the present tense is never completely transferred into higher levels of sensory activation. Emerging realities are cast into linguistic formats before (reflection) and after (expectation) the fact. One's state of momentary awareness has an uncanny way of dissolving into something else. Such a realization need not be the cause of alarm or despair.

It can be a source of relief to know how improbable it is to convey something identically or correctly to someone else. No one can ever fully express what transpires from one moment to next. Privacy matters. What is revealed on the inside may be concealed on the outside, without exact correspondence in either direction. The goal of achieving a state of (total) mutual influence is hindered by the fact that incomplete or partial communication is all that can be actively realized.

Distortions cannot be ruled out: interference, bias, and miscalculation are disruptive mediators.

Interference. At times things go smoothly and nothing gets in the way. At other times, things seem to work out badly, unravel, or go astray. It matters greatly how to deal with external interference in the fulfillment of complex intentions, plans, strategies, tactics, and goals. Social interactions are construed as reality-testing exercises that are subject to a mix of facilitative and subversive influences.

Goal directed aims are subject to mediating factors. Each act of interpretation is subject to reinterpretation form a changing mix of shifting reference points. Therefore, what gets presented by one is relative to how it is represented by everyone else. Cognitive interference occurs when social actors do not see clearly or hear distinctly, or, on a more complex level, are neither touched deeply by the presence of others nor moved to touch in return.

The notion of personal bias is often equated with prejudice in thought, word, or deed. When used in this loose way, it conjures up undesirable or unfavorable images of people with narrow, rigid, or demeaning views of others. Although an act of bigotry certainly reveals strong biases, the term has a more precise range of application in social science literature. A slanted viewpoint involves salient, often unconscious, distortion in the way things are construed, measured, or taken into account. It results from deviations in the way things are added up (overvalued) or left out (undervalued) in the composite equation. The metaphor of a "stacked deck" captures both motivational and cognitive aspects of questionable actions undertaken by those who insist on viewing things according to their own preexisting, even deeply ingrained, predilections.

Multiple standards of evaluation complicate not only the definition of personal bias but the prospects of social resolution. When A views A's actions as unbiased, and B, C, and D construe it quite differently, the likelihood of miscommunication increases, due not just to contested definition but to incompatible standards of evaluation as well. By these standards, bias can be difficult to detect and even more arduous to control. Nor can issues be separated from the way people think about their mental lapses.

Personal beliefs about the integrity of one's own cognitive activity strongly influence the strategies used to minimize faulty attributions and to locate less slanted assumptions. Even if a person tries to guard against making unfair inferences, judgments, or evaluations, a number of other difficulties stand in the way. It can be quite difficult to stop faulty inclinations from occurring once the process is set in motion. If the original basis is recognized as flawed or discredited, causal logic may persist, leading to belief perseverance.

Not all cognitive biases are created equally. Some matter more, linger longer, or damage more severely than others. There is actually no point in striving for some mythical or unobtainable standard of o sheer objectivity or rationality in our direct dealings with others. Interests dictate involvement. No technique or strategy is bias free. Therefore, efforts to remain impartial do not ensure greater accuracy, or neutralize desire or passion, but often foster a numbing stance of indifference or detachment.

The point is not to eliminate biases but to come to terms with them. Of particular relevance are three types of defensive filters that become salient during complex modes of social interaction and slowly diminish personal capacity to appreciate the intrinsic values of what transpires: (a) ideological distortions, (b) ethnocentric priorities, (c) egocentric methods of evaluation and (d) miscalculation.

Ideological Bias. S/O ride the same Badger Bus. When S rides the bus, S just tries to mind S's own business. On one occasion, however, O sat down next to S and started engaging in small talk right away. This didn't bother S because S didn't have to think about anything. Then O started to talk about religion and asked what S thought about the existence of God. O's next question caused the downfall of the conversation. O asked S if S had accepted Jesus as her personal Savior, the Messiah. As S was a Jew, the answer was no. Instead of dropping the subject, O tried to persuade S to believe exactly as O did by pulling out the Bible and reading quotes from the Old Testament that many Jews find offensive. S told O that it was great for O do be deeply involved in religion but S just did not believe as O did—all this with the unspoken assumption that O would drop the subject. O did not but pulled out a flyer from his Bible study class and told S that it was for all people to study the Word of the Lord. When the bus finally pulled into Madison, in silent reflection S concluded that religion is a touchy subject that strangers should avoid.

Ideology may be viewed as a way of looking at the world that is largely closed to inspection from the outside. Because it is impossible to be in the world without acquiring a generalized conception of one's place in the larger scheme of things, an improvised sense of the way things are (or should be, might be, or could be) is automatically acquired along the way. By implicated, some aspects of one's collective vision may be discarded or discredited. Applied language qualifies as ideological insofar as it is used to create public justification for the privileges and perks of favored individuals, groups, and institutions in the social hierarchy.

Ideological discourse is prone to personal errors associated with inadequate feedback and intolerance of reality-testing from as many viewpoints as there are participants or observers. Where monologue triumphs over dialogue, biased individual will undermine the search for truth, cut off options, and reduce alternatives. The pure ideologue pretends to be talking with others but only as a mean of hearing the sounds of his or her own voice. A coercive mix of pretense and contempt toward others hides the weighted value and vested interests of those who insist on giving commands without accepting them in return. The underling intent of such pervasive distortion is to cloak one's real motives in idealized form to gain deference from them.

Personal ideology can be used as a vision to be imposed on others. A massive imposition is coercive and defensive in aspiration. Moreover, it is a slanted vision that tolerates existing inequities and remains utterly indifferent to the deprivation of others. Most important, underlying premises and working assumptions are covered up, taken for granted, and excluded from deliberation. Ideology takes refuge in one-way discourse ("It's true because I say so") rather than two-way dialogue. Hence, the goal of mutual influence is forsaken.

Ethnocentric Bias. S/O lost each other long ago. During child and young adulthood, O was extremely prejudiced, never careful about what was said, and used offensive terms for minority groups. Since they grew up in a small, conservative town, it used to bother S but he never lost sleep over it. However, once S got into an ethnically diverse University, he finally got up the nerve to point out that what O had been saying all along was dead wrong. It did not seem to do much good and two lost contact for a while. Oddly, a great deal of faulty communication can take place over just one issue in question.

Ideological biases are closely linked with the problem of ethnocentrism. Clearly implicated is an inclination to view one's own group as the center of everything and to measure, rank, and rate all others in reference to it. Because everyone is ethnocentric to some degree, the matter is best viewed on a continuum, ranging from little, some, or a great deal of exaggeration in matters of deference (praise) toward outsiders and suspicion (blame) toward outsiders. At issue is a variation of the basic attribution error. Suppose your own values to be widely relevant and applicable to all others rather than the other way around. Much depends on how much psychological distance is placed between ourselves and others.

As ethnocentrism increases, dualisms and schisms legitimate a stance of indifference, avoidance, or disparagement of outsiders. Trouble begins with ethnocentric speech that is in the service of pejorative (negative) expressions about outsiders such as name calling, inaccurate predictions, and systematic insensitivity to the effects of one's actions on others. In effect, a great deal of potentially valuable information is lost when individual distinctions are lumped together in one general category.

Highly ethnocentric codes are divisive. They promote excessive reliance on first person perspective (self as source, other as object), make far too many (unstated, untested) assumptions, encourage scapegoating (affection toward insiders, disaffection toward outsiders), instill loyalty (for your own kind) in exchange for protection from outside intervention, and exaggerate the value of two-valued classifications (friend/foe). Distortion results from biased forms of misclassification and false or mythical categorization.

Egocentric Bias

S/O engage in talks that always seem to go the same way—very predictably. S is a man who always thinks that he is right. S considers what S says to be the right and truthful standard by which everyone else is to be judged (while O doesn't). This is where the entire misunderstanding comes into play. O believes that everyone is entitled to his or her opinion and should be able to discuss disputed matters in a congenial and open manner. When S/O) discus anything, O always lets S explain his opinions. After S has finished his argument, and O doesn't agree with what S has claimed, it is finally O's turn to explain. Unfortunately, O receives dirty looks, sighs, and comments such as "you-are wrong." Such misunderstandings have led to enormous problems. Basically, there is no longer direct contact and there hasn't been for well over a year because O has grown tired of hearing that O is always the one who is wrong.

Egocentric bias is pervasive. Egocentric assumptions are associated with inflated estimates of the degree to which others think or act in the same way as oneself. As a result, alternative options ae easier to discount or rule out. Egocentric styles are linked with the enormous problem of narcissism and host of self-enhancing biases. Self-serving motives are useful in recasting impressions and recollections to produce a more flattering image. Tendencies toward self-enhancement multiply in ego-involving contexts of social appraisal where failure would be threatening. Inflated language covers up negative self-portrayals. Willingness to exploit others is a means to seek power or control. Also coveted is the need to be the center of attention.

A common theme runs through issues—ideological, ethnocentric, and egocentric—derived from cognitive bias. When we are tempted to identify others people as the so-called cause of our own difficulties, it is useful to remind ourselves that they are also the ultimate source of the solution. Curse cannot be easily separated from cure. The main trouble with biased persons is that they are afraid of getting to close to others. Cognitive biases are reflections of personal defenses against the promise and risk of establishing close ties with others.

Miscalculation

S/O are polar opposites. S is a pessimist while O is an optimist. They get along well until sensitive issues arise. S makes a truthful comment but also knows O will disagree, and that gets the debate going. Then S will argue with O by making points and O will give a rebuttal. S/O go in circles trying to convince the other, who in fact does not hear a word. When S listens to O's arguments, it only makes matters S oppose O even more. They are always in a debate; there is never an end or a victor. S/O are used to one another's frustrating views as to suffer almost complete breakdown in conversation. Because each one is unwilling to talk with the other, serious disputes are a way of life. Each conflict ends with one party getting angry and walking away or shutting the other one out. Serious problems (money, friends, family) are never brought up until they reach the maximum level of intensity and any potential solution has passed long ago. This is how all disagreements go.

Excuses and rationalizations pile up after the fact. Skepticism points to misguided situations where people's conceptions are poorly calibrated with nontrivial consequences. Errors, mistakes, lapses, and self-serving miscalculations are likely to go unnoticed at the very point where it is most difficult to recognize them. There may be no visible symptoms that anything has gone wrong. Whatever operates at the outer fringes of conscious awareness, automatic activation, may not be easily fixed.

Motives and resolve may be lacking to go back through complex thought processes to tease apart bits and pieces of invalid information and correct them for any unwanted effect. Faith in one's ability to control misplaced beliefs is undermined where adherence to false propositions proves irresistible. Documented errors, mistakes, and miscalculations should be taken seriously for no other reason that not to repeat them mindlessly or unnecessarily. Human encounters do not have to be error-free or flawless to qualify as efficacious or intrinsically valuable. Excellence is not the same as perfection.

Accuracy motivation matters. Unfounded expectations are often poorly conceived and generally unwarranted. If there is no willingness or inclination to test them out, neither is there any possibility of acknowledging that one is muddled or simply mistaken. Whether it turns out that we are right or wrong, is something we must earn, not merely presume, the right to claim. This is what makes the discovery of error to be valuable as a self-correcting mechanism.

Accuracy motivation leads people to abandon unwarranted expectations. It also diminishes the frequency and magnitude of attributional errors. Moreover, it also facilitates the ability to deal with complex information and to recall expectancy-inconsistent impressions more readily. Finally, accuracy motivation aligns with skillful search for diagnostic information. The test of accuracy takes place, then, at very specific levels of thin slices of expressive and responsive behavior.

One thing seems reasonably clear. We will never run out of messy things to study. In matters of misinformation, fabrication, camouflage, pretense, and cover-up, striving subjects must be quite good at poorly calibrated practices because there is far too much of it to go around. Endless cycles of distortion and disruption make human encounters far more tedious and obscure than they need to be. A complete solution may be out of the question but a measure of relief for the benefits of all who are concerned is certainly possible.

Summary

Safe havens, resources, favorable conditions contribute to social cohesion and cultural solidarity. Matters are complicated. Wealth knowledge in large systems do not filter down, uniformly, to applied knowledge in small systems. Likewise, effective functioning in local communities do not migrate or intersect easily with large institutions. Infinite expanse of collective knowledge, therefore, is neither feasible nor plausible. Socially desirable intentions do not shift away from socially undesirable downfalls. Goal-directed aims must absorb dualistic trajectories: inclusive or exclusive, expansive or contractive. Valued goals and main priorities work together to compensate for devalued loss of stable meanings.

Complex language use enables resilient beings to transform evolved modes of cultural inheritance and fulfill requisite needs for motility, protection, and security from ecological upheavals. Linguistic skills enhance close ties with others. Daily rituals, routines, and projects are counteractive to physical violence by way of symbolic substitutes. Without access to the vitality of stable meaning systems, struggling subjects would be far less able to control their fate. Sense-making practices promote enhanced ability and skill in social interaction.

Constructive arguments engage personal logic for well-reasoned conclusions. Exclusive reliance on argumentative tactics are largely a waste of time. Miscommunication acquires definition in partial or incomplete acts of attempted communication. Goal directed aims are compromised by mixed signals; interference, bias, ideological, ethnocentric, and egocentric indulgence. Miscalculations perpetrate errors, mistakes, lapses, and poor judgment. Accuracy motives are useful as a productive means to minimize protracted disputes and mindless controversy. Human encounters do not have to be error-free or flawless to preserve social knowledge and cultural intelligence.

5

Progressive Achievements

Realistic Standards

People care about daily life. Survive. Rise and shine. Live another day—a precious gift, not to be taken for granted or thrown away. Tomorrow is not a promise. Yesterday is gone, a vestige of fading memory. Only today lingers. Be fully present. Stay alert. Don't wander off. Make the most of opportunity. Minimize constraint. Physical laws never go away. Stay in touch. Keep it real, no pain in the morning, no guilt at night. Progress is measured in small doses. Risk of regression is never far away. Seek shelter, refuge.

Optimum conditions: healthy communication, personal competence, relational compatibility, and symbolic benefits. A sense of sufficiency is a realistic standard by which a good life can be measured along the way. While optimum conditions are not easily achieved, striving subjects may still acquire an enabling surplus of love, care, joy, happiness, interest, and excitement over disabling factors of anger, fear, and sadness.

Progress is measured in small doses. Risk of regression is never far away. Cultivation of physical, emotional, intellectual, and spiritual faith, taken together, foster an abiding sense of wellbeing, growth, and resilience. Mature individuals are more likely to strive for progressive achievements by counting daily blessings than to lament over routine burdens. Pragmatic standards prevail. Invest in what transpires in the present tense. Avoid risks, debts, and entrapments that stand in the way. Slippage into regressive setbacks must be kept at bay. Lofty notions of a life worth living can be secured by living fully every day.

Shared identity promotes social cohesion. General trust in good will of other people affirms the presumption of shared values. In a larger sense, societal solidarity requires a broader array of common priorities: willingness to share assets, collective alignments, and diffuse tendency to enhance civic truth. There is no straight line from personal, relational, or social transfers up the scale to equal investments in abstract notions of cultural benefits. No one poses an infinite capacity to be everything to everyone all the time.

Therefore, meaning systems must be allocated in affordance with specific priorities in daily life. Striving subjects are left to navigate through a precarious world where common values can be taken for granted or thrown aside. Traditional meanings can be called into question at any time or place, particularly from distant or detached observers who reside outside of the web of significance. A same disclaimer applies to faith in inclusive standards without provision for excluded alternatives. Equal concern for insiders and outsiders, may hold for equitable egalitarian principles but not for inequitable wealth distribution. In a world of inevitable contestation, singular assess to scarce resources, multiple appeal to sympathy, empathy, compassion and tolerance will only go so far. Mortality is not inexhaustible.

The power of language occupies middle ground. Rules of social interaction presume that progressive achievements require collective movement away from extreme of radical positions but rather toward collective values of convergence and conjunctive influences. Small-scale systems, far more than large-scale operations, are more likely to benefit. Social cohesion and societal solidarity are more likely to be claimed by social actors who are heavily invested in their own personal concerns. Large-scale institutions work best under impersonal, automatic activities concealed in multiple layers of bureaucratic manipulation.

A unified system is not compatible with divided misalignments. Meaning systems, therefore, do not migrate easily across local, regional, national, or international territories. A fully integrated (egalitarian) society is fashioned through subordinated, segmented links across network boundaries. Multiple forms of social cohesion and cultural solidarity register in active networks of resource allocation. Inclusion reveals social and cultural alignments. Some people are accorded solidarity, others are excluded.

Prevailing notions of social cohesion and cultural solidarity may be construed as aligned features of civility, except for misaligned features of deterioration. Socialization reminds us that the flip side of cohesion and solidarity is the risk of alienation and estrangement. Whatever counts as progressive meaning on the affirmative side of the equation must also, however grudgingly, allow for loss or degradation on the other.

Vital meaning systems are not vulnerable to total disintegration as long as existence is secure. More plausible is personal sensitivity, responsibility, for the common good. However, pervasive inequality, disproportionate allocation of scarce resources, are indifferent to sweeping appeals to the common good, acutely in a landscape of uncommon ill will. Independence (separation) may not easily submit to claims of interdependence (integration).

Claims for diversity can be cause for the vested interests of one community over another. Optimistic concern with the living conditions of other members reside in robust notions of cohesion and solidarity. Acute awareness of the plight of disadvantaged citizens is more difficult to reconcile.

Progressive achievements register across broad spectrums of daily life. Productive gains open up wider latitudes of working agreement and mutual understanding. Conversely, regressive loss tends to narrow latitudes of acceptance and wide latitudes of rejection. By implication, multiple pathways of acceptance, accommodation and convergences may be expected to open up greater provision for social cohesion and cultural solidarity to prevail over opposing forces of alienation and estrangement. A common baseline of personal competence and relational compatibility tends to make room for a rich surplus of working agreements and mutual understandings to prevail over deficient measures of working disagreements and mutual misunderstandings.

Personal competence

It is foolish to reduce notions of personal competence to linguistic facility. Human adaptation requires acute environmental sensitivity. Physical laws penetrate societal boundaries without mediation from applied language. Midwestern citizens endure brutal northern winters rather than migrate to southern comfort. The price is huge. Travelers freeze in snowstorms. Ice fisherman drown in shallow ice from frozen lakes. Deer-car accidents are a leading cause of death at night. Drivers perish from auto accidents on impassible roads. Wooden houses ignite from heated registers. Natural disasters abound. Raging wildfires in Paradise Cl burned life, limb, and property to the ground. Tide waves from Katrina washed everything downstream, houses, cars, and pets. Rising ocean temperatures prevent wealthy condo owners on the southern Florida coast to get flood insurance. Lack of rain affords no relief. Children have suffered in Flint Michigan from toxic water. Invisible aspects of climate change imply visible extinction of once viable human settlements. Grim predictions of a seventh extinction, from ruthless plunder of earthly surfaces, render human escape null and void. Final solutions elude human grasp.

Human encounters can be so disarmingly simple, automatic, and even mindless in one situation and still be so complicated, intricate, difficult, or vexing the next. Daily realities are far too messy to be absorbed in one neat and tidy notion of personal competence. The more complicated an interactive system appears, the more uncertain its state of observation must be. Progressive differentiation of complexity is what makes sustained coordination so difficult to maintain. The same notion holds from the efficacy and effectiveness of social interaction. There is no assurance that social transactions will be certain or trouble fee. Either subject or subject matter can be called into question. Individually constituted and socially constructed meanings must be disentangled for progressive achievements to be sustained.

The study of personal competence must not be allowed to rule out aversive effects of social incompetence. What makes things better cannot be isolated from what makes things worse. The promise of agreement carries the risk of disagreement. The search for understanding may forestalled by the risk of misunderstanding. The struggle for realization may be undermined by failure of realization. Whatever supports shared constructions of credit, currency, and credibility may be later subject to discredit, disqualification, and invalidation.

The ability of one person may not be sufficient to overcome the lack of ability of any other person. Whatever is subject to prior gain is vulnerable to later loss. Human beings are synthetic, wholistic, and integrated entities. Therefore, abilities and skills do not evolve into two separate sense making systems but rather one system that can dissolve into opposite forms. What produces competent behavior on a given day can give way to incompetent behavior the next day.

To keep socially desirable notions of personal competence in check, it is necessary to make room for a spirit of analytic neutrality. The personal competence of one may not be sufficient to override the social incompetence of another. In fact, the competence of one may not compensate for the incompetence of any other. Much depends on whether personal competence is grounded in conditions of adaptation, mindfulness, expressivity, and responsiveness. These four components can be used to explain socially desirable outcomes and to account for how and why engaged persons fall short of the mark.

A sufficiency standard is adaptive across a wide spectrum of engaged endeavors. A realistic stance does not imply steadfast triumph over insufficient setbacks. Personal competence aligns with a state of attentiveness, mindfulness, and focused concern over lapse into a state of inattentiveness, mindlessness, or lack of concentration. There is nothing to prevent competent take out references The desire for mutual influence works best when there is a good fit in stylistic variations of multiple parties. Shared adaptation enhances generous expanse of collective meaning systems.

It is easy to envision progressive achievements where every social actor adapts, adjusts, and accommodates to the stylistic variations of everyone else. Deference and demeanor rule. No one gets out of line. Everyone is gracious, appropriate, accommodating and efficacious. Prior experience intersects with mutual adaptation, emotional stability, achievement motives, and behavior modification. All favor cognitive flexibility, coping skills, and steady response to novel, unusual, or ambiguous task demands. Acquired gains facilitate growth, maturity, and resilient personal change.

Competent persons tend to rely on goal-directed aims that fit well with their own resource base. Effective investments in time, energy, and effort are a refined means to achieve realistic goals and sustain compensatory adjustments to unexpected loss. Striving subjects do not solve social difficulties from scratch. Instead, skillful persons who make informed decision learn to adapt, adjust, and alter behavioral styles on the basis of shared history rather than one-shot choices based on prior trials. Competent behavior depends on rapid decisions that guide shared behavior, aid recall of silent memory, and use of wider search strategies that connect stored information with deliberate choice.

Willingness to discuss negative events greatly enhances stress reduction and rapid adaptation to aversive setbacks. Willingness to recognize discomfort, stress, and tension relieves pressure and improves reliance on useful countermeasure. Expressivity and responsiveness also reduce the impact of intrusive thoughts. Talk about troubles with sympathetic observers also facilitates cognitive reintegration of negative responses into their positive rejoinders. Progressive pathways enable competent participants to fulfill their own distinctive strivings, plans, objectives, and goals.

Guiding principles of self-expression, clear interpretation, and accurate responses may be nurtured, regulated, preserved and enhanced, insofar as strategic factors and tactical maneuvers are securing in play. Cohesive interaction promotes mutual adjustments, insofar as social acts are able and willing to maximize wide latitudes of interdependence and minimize reliance on dependent (submissive) actions or independent (detached) behaviors. Leading indicators: (1) mutual accommodation, (2) mindfulness, (3) expressiveness, and (4) responsiveness.

Mutual Accommodation

S/O are sisters who were raised in an affectionate family. S/O look at the world in the same way. Neither S/O is afraid to talk about what is "really" going on inside their heads—partially because they related to each other so well and partly because they are sisters who have to be forgiving. S/O react to each other with respect. S/O rarely interrupt each other. They take turns talking about problems or plans. S/O talk about everything—they have always been close. Even though they have other friends, no one else could understand the way a sibling can.

S/O met two years ago and they just seemed to click or hit it off. Each one makes an effort to be upbeat and optimistic, even in serious conversation. S/O explore dreams, possibilities, and add new ideas to future plans. They are always open to change, explore options, and take a genuine interest in each other. Smiling and head nodding encourage each speaker to continue. If either one does not agree with the other or has a different point of view, neither one is afraid or intimidated to share a contrasting view. S/O never get defensive or uptight. There is a great deal of respect in their relationship. Humor is added without getting off the track. They never question the motives or honesty of one another. It is refreshing for S to be with O. They have a very special relationship which promotes a high level of agreement about many things. It helps to foster self-esteem and makes S feel privileged to have such a wonderful person in S's life. S/O can always discuss whatever they may feel and always receive an encouraging response.

S/O met during their first semester at the University. S was doing calculus in the den when O walked in and they began to talk. It was one of the oddest things that has never happened to S before—they talked for the next two hours. S felt he had known O forever. They've been the best friends ever since. S/O agree on all fundamental principles. Daily interactions are easy, natural, just seem to flow. They are so alike. They just seem to know that the other is thinking. Silence never seems awkward. S/O are not confrontational. If some discord would arise, it would be dealt with subtly or not even considered worthy of address, out of fear of hurting their relationship. Friendship is built on complete trust and mutual respect. They adore each other—they often complement each other and do things that they know the other does not like doing. There is never any explanation to give, things simply get done.

S/O have been friends since first grade. They were raised in similar families, school systems, common backgrounds, and parental influences. S/O have similar views on politics, relationships, social issues, and future plans. Similar perspectives promote agreeable relations. They feel free to express true feelings because they know each other so well and because they share to many attitudes, beliefs, and interest. Their relationship is very easy-going with little pressure to impress the other, since they know each other so well already. When they get serious, conversation is usually very fluent. Because S/O feel so comfortable, the truth is easier to express about serious topics.

S/O have known each other for the past ten years. Their relationship has grown through good times and bad times. S/O express their feelings openly with each other. Emotional expressions depend on daily moods. S/O are very supportive of each other, almost unconditionally. S/O talk about everything together: careers, boyfriends, husbands, disappointments, expectations, babies, health, parents, families, places they'd love to go, future aspirations, social problems, sports, make up, clothes, homes, garden, death, love, and religion. In few instances where they disagree, they allow each other to have different viewpoints and back off by saying something like "you may be right."

S/O spend the majority of their free time together. This allows them to really work through issues. S/O have long conversations which are always approached with free minds, free of judgment. S/O share similar backgrounds: family, friends, education, relationships, and experience. A common base of shared experience is crucial—they may not be exact, but they are parallel. They can relate subjects back and forth to produce a deeper understanding of key issues. Both S/O become very intensely engaged in conversation. S/O respect each other, really care, and listen to the other's opinion, regardless of the subject. There is no sense of binding agreement, where the other will agree just to agree. Rather, each response is well thought out and felt with great depth. S/O don't feel they always have to agree—they just seem to agree about most of what matters most of all.

S/O have been close friends for thirteen years. S/O never run out of things to say, regardless of how long they have recently talked or when they last saw each other. Conversations flow from one topic to another— often without a transition. S/O can follow each other even when they change subjects. Thoughts and feelings just seem to flow simultaneously. When S talks to O it is almost like S is talking to herself. They can finish each other's sentences. Talk is easy because they don't have to work hard to convey what they are saying. S/O can pick up each other's meanings very easily. Other friends say S/O speak in "stereo" because they share the same styles, word choice, etc. Talk is very comforting because they can always predict the other's response. It is very satisfying to be so reinforced and so well understood.

Mutual accommodation requires shared history, favorable conditions, and convergent meaning systems. Personal styles fit together, without undue friction, strife, or strain. Comfort is reciprocated. Mutuality favors receptivity. Interests coincide. Multiple topics are explored in depth and detail. Motives are rarely called into question. Best of intentions are implied. Strong bonds are privileged as worthy achievements. Personal investments expand, converge, coalesce, in good times and bad times. Serious issues are not taken as impediments. Topics are expansive. Meanings are generous. Tough issues are not avoided but rather serve as a means to work though, resolve, or reconcile on equal terms.

Respect, honesty, and trust align as core values. Negative defenses are displaced in favor of open, free exchange that leaves each partner feeling safe and secure. Mature defenses, humor, pleasure, altruism, and suppressed hostility are conducive to mutual adaptations in daily contacts. Personal interest, narrative exploration, and shared accommodation work together to facilitate high levels of goal attainment. Accumulative gains protect problem solving and preserve cherished meaning systems.

Mindfulness

S/O have been friends for a long time. When they get together, it doesn't matter if they have talked for months, or how much their lives have changed in different ways.

S/O feel as if they've never parted from daily contact, since no barriers or walls were ever felt. S/O want the very best for each other. They feel no competition, express themselves freely, and say exactly what they mean, without worrying about harsh judgments. The biggest thing that helps is that they both listen, really listen. Even through their life experiences are completely different, they have learned from each other in ways that enable them to see the other's perspective more clearly now. It is a very supportive, honest relationship, yet both feel comfortable not sharing as well. S/O can talk about absolutely everything. They have talked about men, cooking, catty women, politics, money, health, morals, sex, and even the weather. S/O talk just to complain about life, to shared exciting news, to relieve boredom, to ask advice or give it, and just to talk.

S/O have known each other for only a few years, yet they interact s if they have truly known each other for a lifetime. S/O can sit and talk for hours: dreams, goals, and steps they want to take in life. This doesn't mean they agree about everything, they do have different views on some things, but both feel that they can always actively and honestly air their separate opinions. A different view enlightens the other and keeps them open-minded and aware of different ways of looking at things.

S/O have always been best friends and they always will be. When they interact, they don't have to say a word to express what they mean. Each one can know what the other is thinking, read expressions like a book and vice versa. S can always tell then O is feeling sad, happy, etc.

even when others can read their minds. This is partially due to the fact that they spend so much time together. S/O live together and see each other on a regular basis. They express themselves very openly. Whenever one has a problem with what the other does, issues of hurt feelings are brought into the open. If something is hurtful, let the other know so things won't build up until someone blows up at the other. S/O treat each other will respect. If S has a serious problem, O will listen and try to help S solve it. O cares about what S does and S cares about what O does. They are always there for each other. Mutuality helps partners come closer because it makes them feel that they are more like themselves.

S/O express themselves freely. Routine interactions are very open. S/O are never worried about what the other will think. They both know the other will agree. S/O use words, gestures, and sometimes they don't have to say anything at all. There is just a look in the eye that tells everything. They seem to know what the other is thinking. S/O react the same way, with nods or shakes of the head. They can even finish each other's sentences. They can talk about everything. When dealing with serious matters, they can cry together too. They try to comfort each other.

They show sympathy. S/O can just laugh at gossip, swap stories, or just complain together.

S/O can always read each other's minds. After long periods of time together, they able to sense what each one is thinking or feeling. S/O have no problems knowing what the other feels or thinks. It is always easy to say what they really want or feel because they know the other normally feels the same way.

S/O have recently gone their separate ways. When they do each other, the bond is still strong, if not stronger than ever. They sill know what the other is thinking or feeling.

S/O could swear they are soul mates. They both have a very caring nature. S/O are able to open up so easily because they have both revealed their insecurities, faults, and failures. S/O trust each other with their deepest secrets. What is going though one's head is what the other knows less by what is going on.

S/O can talk about anything that comes to mind. S/O express themselves openly. They use each other as a source of support. There is no withholding of attempted communication. The mutual expressions of S/O are quite detailed. A great deal of spontaneity is involved. Such agreeable persons are able to discuss problems openly. When disagreement does occur, it does not irritate or frustrate but rather serves as an opportunity to convince the other of the validity of respective viewpoints.

S/O have known each other for six years—at times it seems they can read each other's mind. One may start a sentence and the other will finish it. Neither one takes anything for granted. S/O share a two-way relationship with a lot of give and take. Effective communication has developed over time because they really work at it. S/O work had to overcome barriers that stand in the way. As time goes by, they change and so do their daily encounters just as well.

Acts of accommodation and mindfulness are interchangeable. Personal differences are easy to reconcile. Daily encounters give rise to gradual expansions of aligned meaning systems. Core values align. Conversation is described in much the same way: open, fluid, flowing, across issues large and small. Observers and participants are fully present. Topics multiply without end. Safety and security rule the day. The main difference is greater stress on mind-reading in the mindfulness section. Empathy, trust, sensitivity increase confidence that each one knows what the other is thinking or feeling, whether comfort or discomfort rise to the surface or are covered up underneath conscious awareness.

Mutual mindfulness follows from a long tradition of shared history and convergent styles of expression and response. Shared knowledge can be preserved indefinitely, come what may. There is everything to discuss and every way to say it. Daily contacts range from hard work to easy play. It does not matter how much time has passed from the las direct encounter, through unspecified periods of presence and absence. What remains is an enduring symbolic sense that heavily invested partners have never really parted. The

Lingering effects of mutual mindfulness need not dissipate over time. It is possible to be fully present in periods of protracted absence or separation of close bonds. It takes two separate, distinctive sources to construct a tight connection that endures over time. No artificial obstacles, barriers, or impediments are allowed to stand in the way. Mindful exchanges, over tangible subjects and intangible references, may remain vibrant, alive, or vigorous, without constant or periodic reinforcement.

Narrative themes are long lasting, and unfold against standards of sufficiency to transcend time and place of origin or destination. Timeless bonds are within reach, as long as memories, reflections are kept alive. An abiding climate affords comfort and calm, despite distance or displacement. Affectionate parties may vow to be always there for each other. The promise of kindred spirits may merge into one. Mutual mindfulness, therefore, has a spiritual force that never fails.

Expressiveness

S/O express their true feelings. S/O never hide their true feelings. They say what is on their mind just about all the time. S/O have very open minds. It is important not to be assume the worst or have negative feelings until each one has a chance to explain. S/O expect each other to be open and honest about sensitive feelings. If something is wrong, it is important to take care of it right away. If one makes the other feel bad or upset, the only way to feel better is to tell the other so they can work it out.

S/O express themselves openly, whether the subject is negative or positive. They respect their friendship. They place emphasis on shared honesty. S/O see many aspects of life through the same eyes. They share new ideas openly. When S/o talk, they listen and talk until they both can affirm that no meaning has been lost. S/O never run out of things to say. They are strong people who listen, grow, and learn from each other. S/O work hard at communicating well.

S/O can read each other's minds. They share high levels of trust which affords the freedom in the way they express differing opinions. S/O can finish each other's sentences.

They are willing to listen and put themselves in the other's shoes. S/O have the ability to focus on what the other says or does. They are open to suggestions, even if it differs from their own. S/O strive to learn about themselves, each other, and the relationship as a whole. They want to keep learning and growing from helpful interaction. When S/O interact, they encourage and show genuine concern for one another's welfare.

S/O have been good friends through many years. They interact on a daily basis. S/O related well and this allows them to talk openly and freely about various problems. There is never a strain or discomfort in conversation. S/O can always talk about personal problems without difficulty. All along, whether serious or funny, daily interactions are great. S/O get along perfectly and that is why they are such good friends.

S/O have been good friends for fifteen years. They have been through many ups and downs together. O knows S better than anyone maybe even better than O knows herself. O tells S everything. When they talk, it is almost as if they have a coding system or special language. S doesn't even have to finish many sentences. They almost always come to the same conclusion, if not, they can persuade the other to see things in a similar way. S/O have a similar style in the way they feel about life decisions, education, politics, relations, and family. When S/O get together, they just have this bond that connects them, despite all outside confusion from others. They are very open. Maybe this is why it works so well.

S/O have interactions that are never forced. They can talk about anything. S/O discuss politics, religion, money, the poor, especially education, and the future of the world. S/O never hold back their opinions about anything. They rarely disagree. S/O say what they are really feeling. They can discuss things with each other that they can't mention to anyone else. S/O discuss problems when they appear and they don't try to ignore them and hope they go away.

S/O can talk for hours about almost anything. They are similar in so many ways and enjoy the same things. S/O enjoy each other's company. They feel good about talking to each other. S/O interact openly on a regular basis.

A major test: whether sensations, perceptions, and conceptions can be expressed in a spontaneous, fluent, and articulate manner. Message production and message reception depends on the same viable features of verbal intelligence. What registers is the capacity to make rapid, accurate, and detailed sense of what transpires along the way. Speed of transfer, rapid recall, short-term memory, and fast reactions enable expressive, literate persons to transform shared activities into narrative themes that are directly accessible to one another. Verbal intelligence, emotional intelligence, intellectual intelligence blend together with nonverbal sensitivity to set boundary conditions for progressive gains to remain securely in place. Expressive freedom is subject to empirical test as a way of initiating and responding to what transpires in the present tense.

An expressive orientation works to promote a spirit of immediacy, creativity explorative inquiry, playfulness and self-actualizing tendencies. Spontaneity is manifest as energy that cannot be stored, recalled, or imitated. It must be released in a short burst, moment-by-moment, and consumed quickly. An immediacy orientation is counteractive to obsessive, compulsive tendencies, dwelling on the past, planning for the future. Impulsive acts do not qualify as spontaneous. Neither does undue reliance on habits or scripts. Mutual spontaneity qualifies as a critical factor by granting social agents some measure of greater control over interdependent connections and reduce reliance on prior outcomes or future predictions. Emotional repression gets in the way. Volition trumps coercion. Shared discovery of emotional freedom is a mutual reward for a strong measure of intrinsic value.

Responsiveness

S/O are compatible. They live together, share common interests, enjoy healthy foods, love to roller blade, work out in the gym, and talk a lot about family and friends. Both S/O have been through rough times and often use each other's shoulder to cry on. Often S/O just need to listen and keep quiet. All the time they have known each other, they have need had a fight. Most times S/O are together, they just spend time laughing.

S/O are sisters who are very comfortable with each other. They can talk about anything. S/O agree about almost everything. When they go shopping, they go in the same store. S/O like the same clothes, music, people, so they have a lot to discuss. S/O can express themselves openly and easily. When one talks, the other agrees. They have the same tastes in food, clothes, movies, music,

TV shows, etc. S/O can talk about anything they want. When they see each other face-to-face, they always smile at each other first. They both start talking at the same time because they always have so much to say. S/O can both tell when something is wrong right away. Just a look on a face can tell something bad has happened or something good has happened. They take turns talking, but sometimes they get too excited and talk at the same time.

S/O are friends who are now away from home. S is from Texas now in Wisconsin and O is at Colorado. It is as if they haven't been separated whenever they talk. They still talk at least three times a week. They are the first person either one can share everything. S/O are the kind of friends who can finish each other's sentence and they always know that the other is thinking. They never hesitate to question any subject, no matter how perverted, twisted, or unusual the topic. They can discuss it at length and never think of each other as queer for asking it. Even though they were only friends for one year before they parted, their relationship is ten times more powerful than the ones with people S has known all her life. They will always be close because they are so similar and understand each other. S/O have gone through similar family problems and this among other similar backgrounds brings them closer together.

Precise alignment of expressive and responsive styles, under favorable conditions, serve to heighten the pleasure of conversation, immediacy orientation, strong elation, and smooth flow of topic shifts. The pace of speech acts may be so engrossing that engaged participants strive to remain so intensely involved in mesmerizing activity that nothing else matters. Derived gains are so pleasurable that close partners will remain totally engaged, even at great cost. Flowing sensations combine acute awareness of effortless concentration, intrinsic motivation, loss of distinction between behavior and environment, merging of body boundaries, loss of temporal awareness, novel responses to challenge, and an upsurge of feelings of competence and freedom.

Such deep, intense involvements in difficult tasks do not overwhelm applied skill, but rather sustain an intense sense of shared exhilaration that is long cherished as an ideal embodiment of shared realities. Total absorption activates a renewed sense of discovery and creative inquiry. Optimal states of mutual attunement in the distribution of expressive and responsive acts combine to produce an elevated sense of authentic connections, as sustained by fruitful and productive endeavors that generate intrinsic rewards without conscious calculation of rewards and costs.

In sum, mutual resolve to get along well can be intoxicating. Engaged subjects forfeit emotional suppression, as a means of giving only surface or simplistic attention to critical issues for the sheer sake of impression management. Instead, involved parties take turns speaking and listening, to give each member a deeper, richer, and more compelling grasp of what transpires across the uneven course of relational history. Progressive achievements, based on accommodation, mindfulness, expressivity, and responsivity, are magnified in social settings where volitional participation prevails over coercive manipulation.

Interpersonal Compatibility

S/O share a good deal of openness with each other. S/O share intimate secrets and they are able to tell each other virtually everything. To achieve such closeness requires a great deal of trust and mutual agreement. S/O express themselves in the same open manner. When there is a problem, S/O want to talk it out. They aren't the type of persons who just want to ignore a problem and let it pass. S/O prefer to sit down and talk things over. They recognize each other's moods just by the way they express themselves.

S/O spend a great deal of time together. Their expressions are completely uninhibited. S/O never feel the need to watch what they say or do. S/O are completely comfortable saying whatever comes naturally. Silence is comfortable. They do not always need to talk to each other. S/O talk but do not argue. S/O are respectful. They save their comments and advice for when the other is finished. Most of what they say is humorous, but they can both tell when the other has something serious to discuss. S/O talk about their futures. When either one is sad or in a bad mood, the other will cheer and laugh things up. When either wants to be alone, no words need to be said. They don't intrude on each other's affairs. Everything they express they do so of their own volition.

S/O trust each other not to repeat what is said or give bad advice.

S/O are best friends who hardly disagree about anything. They have achieved a strong bond together, with shared tendency to almost always agree with each other. They have similar tastes in clothing, food, boys, girls, how friends should treat others, and what a true friend says or does. S/O do not talk down or treat each other with disrespect. They are on equal levels and are fair on all matters. They match or click. S/O tend to analyze situations a bit too much, but it's fun when they engage in deep thinking together. S/O give the best advice. They rely on each other for almost anything. Even at times when they have different opinions, they seem to compromise and make each other feel good by finding a happy medium.

S/O have been best friends since eighth grade. They get along so well because they are so similar. S/O are pretty religious, share qualities of kindness and generosity. They like the same sports, share similar views on world issues and politics, and most of all they love to joke around and act crazy and goofy. However, they are also serious. On several occasions they have stayed up all night talking about relationships, personal goals, dreams, plans for summer, the list for summer, and the list goes on forever. They can talk about anything. S/O can't remember a time when they didn't feel comfortable sharing what was on their mind. They are not afraid to express their opinions. S/O are open and honest with each other, knowing that they will accept and understand anything the other has to say. S/O are energetic, enthusiastic, and playful. They know joking around is superficial. It's great to be able to get into intellectual conversations and know they will back each other 100%. They are very much like a team. They help each other out in tough times. There is a lot of giving rather than taking. S/O speak their minds, but never pressure the other to go one way or another.

S/O are best friends. The two of them are like one person. They shared common ideas, views, and goals. Whenever S needs advice, she turns to O who always knows what to say to make S feel better. S/O always want the best for each other and will do anything to make each other happy. O is a very honest person who will tell S bluntly if S is right or wrong. O helps S learn new things every day. When something good or bad happens to S, O will be the first person to know. Not only does S tell O everything, but also every single detail, including names, dates, times, etc. Their relationship will last a lifetime.

S/O have known each other for eight years. They have never had any major disagreements. S/O are not emotional, very little gets to them, and most situations are brushed off and forgotten. Since both do not care about little picky things, they get along so well. S/O know not to waste time worrying about trivial matters. They are adventurous, spontaneous, and unemotional. If S/O are ever in a situation where disagreement is possible, they quickly recognize the issue and move on to a compromising solution. With compromise achieved so easily, they are able to agree time and time again. S/O will remain friends forever.

S/O are open. They aren't afraid to tell each other exactly how they feel. S/O are considerate of each other. Even when they get upset, they remain courteous, express true feelings, because they have so much respect for each other. When they express themselves, they take into consideration what the other will think or feel. S/O talk about very intimate details in life and share almost everything. They enjoy sharing their thoughts, listen carefully, because they like and understand each other so much. They help each other understand problems and confide in each other on a day-to-day basis.

S/O spend a lot of time together. They are closest friends. S/O never run out of things to say. S/) go for long walks and they are always talking. They have a lot in common. S/O always try to support each other and give good advice. When they do disagree, they are good at explaining why. They always laugh and have a good time, no matter what they do.

There is mystery in what makes people compatible. Competence does not always lead to compatibility. Personal competence acquires definition in the cultivation of resource, ability, and skill. Human encounters involve collective pursuit of intentions, interpretations, structures, functions, and outcomes. Intentions are realized in motives, plans, and goals. Interpretations are activated in perspective taking activities that assign priorities and possibilities in an open field of alternative courses of action. Structure emerges through (large-scale) strategies and (small-scale) tactics that frame or organize emerging activities. Functions are means to ends. Outcomes are designed to fulfill intentions. Definitions of compatibility go well beyond competence measures.

In human encounters, five levels of complexity are embedded in complexity and complication: a coherence standard for sense-making effort; a relevance standard for relational coordination;

a pragmatic standard for strategies and tactics; a relational standard for mutual influence; and a satisfaction standard for short-term outcomes and long-term consequence. Intentional urges are made explicit so multiple parties can read multiple motives. This means the participants can express themselves clearly (coherence standard). Expressive initiatives are followed by closely aligned responses and access each other accurately (relevance standard). Structures exhibit properties of synchrony and alignment. This means the participants can produce well organized sequences of mutual exchange (relational standard). Strategies and tactics are function. This means participants can work well together in an efficient manner (pragmatic standard). Each one may also contribute to the maximum fulfillment of desirable ends and minimize production of undesirable outcomes (satisfaction standard). Effective communication requires that coherent, relevant, pragmatic, relational, and satisfaction measures are subject to complete realization. Complete realization is symptomatic of miscommunication (incomplete standard).

A good fit between competence and compatibility is not assured. Consider relational alliances where mature and literate persons are capable and willing to foster close ties with each other. Person A and person B appear (at first) to get along just fine. In another social context, person C and Person D also get along just fine as well. So far, we have two pairs of congenial partners who have already established, maintained, and cultivated close, affectionate, and intimate bonds with each other. Then one day, perhaps by chance, person B meets person C or person A meets person D under initial conditions of strong mutual attraction. The initial sets of mutual attraction are now subject to social comparison. Now what once seemed exemplary, honorific, or as distinctive measures of relational commitment is now, inexplicably, called into question or found wanting.

Suppose that A and B reach a point of relational dissolution and C and D, for different causes and reasons, also reach a point of relational termination. Under two comparable cases of (initial) affiliation, the end result is exactly the same. Whatever once seemed stable, secure, or firm is subject to radical upheaval. Perhaps implicit signs of potential dissolution (poor fit) were present during initial stages of relational attraction, but not in any way that that was apparent or self-evident at the time. In a strange twist of fate, A commits to C and B commits to D. These transfers occur when a first marriage leads to divorce and then followed by remarriage. What A and B once cultivated as an affection relation soon fell apart. In short, neither measures of competence nor compatibility lasted very long. Both partners found others to fill in the gaps. Marriage, divorce, and remarriage give rise to striking implications.

Assumptions of competence and compatibility are either firmly validated or slowly dissolved along the way. Presumptions are rarely settled (once and for all) but are rather subject top constant change. Tentative notions follow: (1) personal competence does not necessarily lead to relational compatibility. Individual competence may be a necessary but insufficient (pre) condition for relational compatibility. Prevailing notions can be undermined at any time. (2) competence and compatibility may be transformed into their complementary opposites. What once was viewed as favorable or optimal achievement are subject to dissolution, despite the best of intentions or the worst of outcomes. (3) a competent and compatible state of affairs may dissolve into aversive conditions that are disavowed by rejected or excluded partners.

Clearly, firmly grounded and closely aligned human bonds may not prove to be sufficiently resourceful to preserve optimal conditions once they have been established on a firm foundation. Whatever is gained in affectionate alliances may be subject to irretrievable loss. A wide spectrum of personal disputes and dense linguistic entanglements have great potential to unfold over time, sometimes without cause of reason in slight. Linguistic difficulties are likely to multiply in unfavorable, unstable, or unsettled social alliances. The ineffective use, misuse, and abuse of words and gestures are fully implicated in signs of dislocation on all sides.

Personal competence and relational compatibility must be validated and protected from all alarm. Power, affection, and involvement help to explain matters of strength, degree of affiliation, and depth of personal engagement. A broad latitude of interdependence (egalitarian levels of mutual influence) is a critical indicator the total strength of relational commitment. An enduring state of mutual interdependence means that both parties want more of the same thing, namely high levels of shared power (positive sum), a strong surplus of positive affection, and abiding desire to preserve strong levels of collective engagement. For preservation of strong ties, the total latitude of mutual interdependence must be greater than the sum of dependent (submissive) or independence (distance). Shared resources promote a strong sense of common ground. Goal-directed aims are designed toward the fulfillment of welcome outcomes or desired ends.

Summary

Progressive achievements strengthen meaning systems. Realistic standards of sufficiency measure the resilience of a disciplined way of life. Physical, emotion, intellectual, and spiritual growth, taken together, foster well-being and resolve to affirm the best way forward. Count opportunities rather than lament burdens. A worthy life can only be secured by living fully every day. Human encounters cultivate social cohesion. Societal solidarity requires a broader array of shared resources.

The power of language enables mutual movement away from extreme or radical outlooks in favor of shared tolerance of convergent values, moderation, and consensus formation. Principles of inclusion unify; those of exclusions divide. Regard for the living standards of other members align with robust values of cohesion and solidarity. The plight of disadvantaged citizens is difficult to reconcile. Progressive gains promote wide latitudes of working agreement and mutual understanding. Regressive loss produces narrow latitudes of acceptance and wide margins of rejection.

The tension between competence and compatibility must be disentangled for progress to be achieved. Competence makes things better. Incompetence makes things worse. Personal capabilities are grounded in affirmative conditions of accommodation, mindfulness, expressivity, and responsiveness. Shared willingness to confront negative outcomes tends to enhance stress reduction and minimize regressive setbacks.

Mutuality is based on shared history, favorable inquiry, and aligned meaning systems. Regressive defenses are displaced in favor of free, open exchanges that leave social agents feeling safe and secure. Mindfulness is able to reconcile personal differences. Shared knowledge can be preserved infinitely. Timeless bonds are protected as long as active memories, reflections, and hope are kept alive. Expressivity registers as the capacity to process information rapidly, accurately, precisely, in detail.

Verbal, conceptual, and emotional intelligence blend together with nonverbal sensitivity for meaning systems to expand outward in diffuse trajectories across the cultural landscape. Responsiveness certifies accuracy. Progressive alignments, accommodation, mindfulness, expression, and response, are magnified in congenial settings where volitional participation prevails over coercive manipulation. Competence activates resource, ability, and skill. However, competence does not ensure compatibility, unless there is a good fit in personal and social styles of presentation and reception. Progressive aspirations are designed to fulfill welcome outcomes and desired ends.

6

Strong Bonds

Attachment Risk

Neither strong bonds nor intimate attachments are mandatory features in daily events. In crowded locations, social transactions take place in fleeting contacts with strangers who will never be seen again. A stance of anonymity, indifference, or resignation need not be labor intensive. Strangers go unnoticed. No one needs to notice anyone else. Mingling does not imply intention.

Isolated subjects fulfill routine tasks by themselves. Isolation need not rely on familiar rituals. Nor is it necessary to obey rules, roles, or norms where they do not apply. Fleeting exchanges do not last long. People, places, and things fade away in dense settings where no one cares about anyone else.

Brief exposure to strangers reduces a need for adaptation to customs of deference and decorum. Demand features are neutralized where there is nothing to be gained or lost. Simply pass by. Go unnoticed. The only satisfaction is to be left alone. Avoid dense traffic at rush hour. Avoid long lines.

Avoid congestion. Don't pick up the phone, answer the door, or check e-mail. Absence is better than presence of pretense. Faulty contacts can be worse than no contact at all. Social activity may be less attractive than dedication to a lost cause. Futility lingers where nothing is gained but a waste of time.

Isolated persons avoid messy affairs that are over as soon as they begin. Freedom to move away is not a mandate for freedom to stay. Freedom to stand outside of misery and mayhem (in a violent world) may give rise to a broader appreciation of what it means to be trapped inside with no way out (to the outside). Stay away from large-scale systems of oppression and exploitation that deny access to negotiation or mediation. Subsistence wages do not afford escape from tedium or drudgery. Avoidance of coercive attachments may afford relief from unjust treatment.

Strong bonds are valued where human attachments are welcome or desired. Selective access to strong bonds does not displace weak bonds in risk-reward calculations. Acquisition of strong bonds are socially desirable where appreciation of one's place in the larger scheme of things align with favorable conditions, realistic standards, affirmative activity, and collective knowledge. By extension, weak bonds are better than none. In safe and secure relations, labor-intensive effort prepares the way for striving subjects to protect and nurture affectionate alliances. In general, a rich surplus of working agreements and mutual understandings must be reality tested as a means to withstand brief episodes of disagreements or misunderstandings. Strong attachments allow conjunction and convergence (common ground) to prevail over divergence and disjunction.

Working Agreement

S/O have learned to read each other's reactions, facial expressions, body language accurately. Mutual respect enables them to reach solid agreements. S/O can sense the desires (best interests) of each other. They are able to interpret each other in a sensitive manner. Often, they can predict each other's response to stressful situations as a useful way to avoid conflict. They take care to listen fully to each other's viewpoints on critical issues. After they take time to consider each situation, they reach the same conclusion on their own. They share the same values, interests, and ideas which makes it easy to reach mutual agreement.

S/O engage in deep conversations. Living together as close friends enables them to talk about everything and anything. S/O share similar beliefs, attitudes, and morals. They stay in close accord along with a spirit of regard and respect. S/O enjoy interactions that are pleasurable, informative, and lots of fun.

S/O have known each other for seven years. They have always been able to communicate well because of mutual interests and general outlooks on life. S/O share the same love of travel, art, cycling, movies, and moral values. They share mutual understanding of where each one is going in life. They know each other well enough to be able to read each other's tone of voice, facial expressions, and hand gestures. S/O don't have to convince the other how they feel because it is already understood. It is exciting to have someone who listens to what you are saying, stay interested, and respond intelligently. They are true believers in active listening as a vital part of a strong relationship. S/O are close friends who have always been able to communicate well.

S/O are close friends. Conversations promote strong levels of mutual agreement. They are about the same age and place in life, both married with children, and they have careers outside the home. S/O's personalities are similar, easy going, get along well with others, with a tendency toward optimism. Their backgrounds are similar. They were raised in middle class, two-parent homes where the mother stayed home with the children. The only difference is that O lived in a rural setting, whereas S lived in the city. Face-to-face contact takes place most often in one of their homes while the children, all boys, play together in another room while they drink tea and talk at the kitchen table. S/O choose to be together, leaving behind other things they should be doing at the time. Conversations are a reprieve from the rigors of ordinary life. They cover a wide range of topics. They move past surface levels right into things that matter most to them. S/O verbalize opinions, feelings, hand gestures, and facial expressions to illustrate their points. They look directly at each other and pause if there is any interruption. Without missing a beat, they go right back to where they were. Regardless of subject, S/O take turns to express themselves while the other listens intently. They accept each other's viewpoints. They explore every angle, ask questions, and restate the points they feel most deeply. S/O) sigh heavily, silently nodding, ready to move on to another subject. At all times they stay relaxed. There is no concern about putting on airs. They are free to say it like it is without ever worrying about how it will sound. With lots of humor, laughter is sprinkled through conversation to break up the intensity. Conversation continues right up to the point where one person backs out of the driveway to go home. They leave wishing there had been more time to talk.

S/O interact every day. They enjoy each other's company. S/O feel comfortable together. What first brought S/O together was mutual love for time spent together, biking, hiking, waterskiing, snowboarding, or camping. Whenever they did these things, they usually did them together and enjoyed the fun of being together. They are always helping each other learn new techniques or pushing the other to higher levels. When interacting with others, they are approached with initial respect. If their ideas do not agree with those of others, they still try to respect other's viewpoints. S/O value happiness over money; if they are always working there is no time for play. S/O have fun together and feel comfortable being together because they agree so much. It's not that they agree about everything, but they do agree on the most fundamental issues of life.

S/O are compatible because they have the same guidelines in life. S/O have similar qualities in the way they handle social situations. They feel that friends, family, and fun are the most important things in life. S/O can talk about everything. They want the same things out of life. S/O are very easy persons to get along with; sensitivity and caring of others enables them to open up to each other. S/O share the same priorities. If one has a problem, the other one knows how to make the other feel better. S/O agree about shared aspects of life: balance between diet and exercise, religion, friends, family, school, love, sex, marriage, selflessness, respect, honesty, loyalty, and responsibility. S/O share the highest possible levels of shared agreement.

S/O are best friends who know how to react to each other; they always see things eye-to-eye. They talk about something small and progress to larger issues. S/O are polite, and interested in what either one has to say--it is usually on par with what the other is thinking. They ask a lot of questions because they really enjoy hearing what the other has to say. They make fun of themselves a lot. It is enjoyable, fun, and reassuring to hear other people talk about their problems without whining but rather laughing at them. Friendly teasing allows them to be comfortable with each other.

S/O were drawn to each other right from the start. They both have a stake in finding common ground that feels precious and delicate. S/O have avoided some issues they sense might have provoked disagreement. When inevitable differences do arise, they find ways to laugh and tease. Their friendship means too much to let talk separate them. S/O agree to disagree gently, without judgment. Being right is not critical. They both feel free to change their minds about something without conceding a victory. Agreement is a function of careful listening and viewing issues from a different angle. Often what appears at first to be a disparate point of view turns out to be a function of semantics, but they take the time to find out.

S/O agree on just about everything. When they get home at the end of the day, they sit at the kitchen table, talk, and listen. S/O always seem to have enough time to listen to each other bitch about hassles, friend, or the opposite sex. They always know where the other stands. They are never far apart. Underneath shared agreements is a deep respect for each other as distinct individuals. S/O are open with each other. S/O help each other realize how they want to live. They laugh with each other every day. They agree because of openness, caring, and respect for who they are as women.

S/O are best friends who don't hold secrets from each other. They are very open, honest, and know a lot about each other's way of life. S/O react in a positive manner. They give advice and help each other relate problems to similar past experience. S/O talk about almost everything: academics, grades, friends, social life, parents, and backgrounds. If they are not in agreement, they discuss it at length. Generally, either one will change a position so they agree how to handle a particular problem. They come to agreement not to change each other's mind, but because they hear idea or views that may sway their own. S/O talk about anything that matters to them. They share so much agreement because they are very similar and open to the other's view.

Human relations flourish when goal-seeking participants are able and willing to secure a broad base of working agreements with one another. It is a mistake to view the completion of daily tasks, habits, and routines as conducted in a dull, dry, droning, or dispassionate manner. Personal agreements are not achieved, it turns out, in the manner of a bean-counting exercise. To the contrary, strong emotions are implicated across a broad spectrum of specific effects and protracted outcomes.

Mutual constructions of working agreement often evoke strong positive sentiments (love, joy, happiness), whereas mutual construction of complex working disagreement often arouse an equally salient range of negative sensibilities (anger, fear, sadness) in response. In performative terms, the active sense of doing well yields to elation and eagerness while the sense of doing poorly gives way to sadness and depression or, in cases of avoidance, to anxiety and fear.

Social agents who score highest on scales of agreeableness are often viewed as being moderate, tender-minded, sensitive, cooperative, and disposed to praise others than simply praise themselves.

A style of agreeableness and warmth is linked to trait measures of a strong relational orientation. As a rule, explicit displays of warmth register on the brighter and lighter side of social entanglements. A congenial stance of acceptance, agreeableness, assertiveness, and warmth fosters more lenient ratings of others. An agreeable disposition portends less routine conflict but more emotional distress when it does occur than is true of less agreeable counterparts.

The potential for consensual agreement is robust. In a cyclical equation, persons who agree seek individuals who agree easily, and, thereby each one acquires a tacit base of constructive expectations and a refined means to reproduce or renew favored conditions. In contrast, individuals who score highest on scales of disagreeableness appear to others as being pompous, conceited, egocentric, competitive, antagonistic, skeptical, critical, or distrustful toward rivals.

Agreeableness has a close affinity with reproduction of favorable impressions, pleasant responses, ranking of liking, and willingness to submit or yield to the controlling influence of other persons. Social inconsistency does occur, of course, when people confront demands that go against deeply ingrained or habitual strivings. Another countervailing influence stems from the fact that cordial and congenial styles of self-presentation can be faked or feigned, despite risks of appearing too compliant or overly cheerful. It does not require a clever or adroit person to project a contrived sense of sincerity, concern, or regard to seek favor from other people.

Strategic acts of feigned sincerity constitute the heady stuff of which all manner of nonsense and chicanery can be used as a clever disguise or convincing illusion transformed by word manipulation into a deceptive or magical pose of pretense, artifice, or fabrication. A false sense of amicability and ingratiation, together with a strong self-enhancing, social desirability pressure, can be troublesome as a result of the value assigned to politeness, friendliness, compliance, and tolerance in daily life.

As a baseline of shared agreement moves from simple to complex status, the sheer number, complexity, and scope of appraisal standards are likely to increase in difficulty, scale, and scope as a result. For these reasons, people differ in what they are capable and willing to agree about, as do shared conditions in which such mutual discoveries can be reaffirmed, disconfirmed, or discarded. Those who deal effectively with complex subject matter are best able to form well-organized perspectives and act skillfully in difficult situations. Capacity to underscore positive events with others is linked with constructive attitudes, beliefs, moods, and enhanced sense of well-being; active responses enhance benefits of intimacy and satisfaction.

Signs of mutual affection and binding agreement often blend, fuse, merge when each member feels valued, cared and appreciated in daily life. Attraction and attachment generate greater motives for direct access to selected persons who are accorded preferential and deferential treatment as sources of protection and security. Mutual agreement also serves as an effective antidote to strong anger or suppressed hostility. Large-scale agreements fall into place as the basis for strength of relational ties. In a word, consensual agreements are an important source of social capital and afford psychic protection against corrosive effects of wear, tear, stress and strain.

Narrative themes follow in turn: recognition of intent, common perspective, complimentary identities, similar interest, compatible values, quality of interaction. Direct encounters are sustaining, sufficient, reaffirming, and successful. Working agreements are well grounded in elaborated meaning systems and refined stockpile of social knowledge. Virtually anything can be brought to the table--worries, problems, dreams, troubles, secrets, interests, values, beliefs, attitudes, moods, goals, plans, and envisioned futures.

Close bonds and strong attachments are mutual productions. Working agreements promote meaningful constructions. High quality encounters are linked to shared ability and mutual willingness to agree about the way things are. Creative inquiry opens up new ways of thinking, feeling, behaving, and relating to others. Conversations flow when sensory activities are shared across congenial alliances. Speaking and listening styles are better tolerated when strength mingles with weakness.

It becomes easier to detect subtle differences freely and confront touchy issues. Success occurs insofar as one source is able to interpret the intended meanings of another person's actions. Mutual effectiveness enables the vocabulary of one person to be translated into the lexicon of another person. An intuitive grasp of what is implied requires hard work and concerted effort rather than merely presented as self-evident. Also relevant to dynamic exchange is the ability to detect unstated urges, often without a word being spoken.

Intentions may resister at the outer fringes of conscious awareness. Mutual effort to grasp implied intentions can lead to greater appreciation for the sheer complexity of desire, intention, and purpose. Fluent speakers and alert listeners learn how what to express and what to leave out. Unspoken convergence relies on staying in touch with hidden rules and make implicit notions explicit, without having to spell everything out in precise detail.

Clear recognition of personal intent is linked with acute awareness of shifting states or mood changes. Good observers stay alert to the meaning of silence, the unspoken, what is left out of verbal cues. What emerges is a profile of mutual effort to recognize goal-directed aims to tolerate ambiguity and uncertainty that comes along the way. Tolerance of what goes wrong is a means to make it go right.

Working Disagreement

The difference between agreement and disagreement cannot be reduced to positive (+) or negative (-) signs. An act of agreement adds to what an act of disagreement subtracts. However, subtraction is more intense, salient, and lasting. Destructive acts have more impact than their constructive counterparts. Negative disaffection may be limited to trivia, small talk, and minor irritation or escalate from tension, irritation, annoyance, aggravation to hostility, frustration, anger, jealousy, and hate. Intense repetition can also spin out of control, from hot anger, to verbal abuse, and verbal fights. Wounds and injuries are not easily healed and sometimes not at all. Even strong attachments unravel when a surplus of working agreement is squandered and dissolved in a downward spiral.

S/O engage in talks that end up badly. S will say "I can't discuss this with you because you are too closed-minded. O will refuse to listen because O talks about the way things were in the past and why he did something a certain way back then. Next, when S tries to explain that what worked in the past won't work now. O retorts with a question. "Why it won't work now?" From that point, S and O get into a cycle of anger and resentment, even when S realizes where they are heading and tries to stop it. The process also works in reverse. O is sure each one thinks that he is doing everything to get his point across, but he is simply looking from his point of view and S is doing the same.

S/O try to talk about touchy subjects, then one or the other will get angry, and they end up in a shouting match. S/O get angry because they hate arguing and they can't seem to stop it. S/O never agree about anything—slowly O learns the only reactions that O is going to get from S are a toxic combination of anger and tears. S/O talk, but O avoids talking about what S is describing. O acts exasperated and frustrated, sighs very heavily, and walks out leaving S very angry. S/O try to talk, but S shuts O out with harsh, mean words that do not help O understand S's point of view. S/O have shot, hostile, or cold conversations; they are often angry about things that have happened in the past that have not been confronted—because these implicit angry feelings are often left unspoken; their interactions are hostile and they often do not know why. S/O have hurt each other in horrible ways—they let little things drive them apart; they have become infatuated with their anger and stubbornness. S/O are complete opposites; talks usually turn into bitter fights; they get defensive and jump to conclusions; they are hostile whenever they talk; they get angry very easily—they are never relaxed or comfortable, and they always have their guard up. S/O find that sometimes O makes S so angry that S doesn't care to see O for days at a time—when they are together, they are always yelling or talking very loudly. S/O become very angry with each other— level of anger depends on how much S thinks O is watching his mouth and how patient S is; they have crossed the line many times before. S/O get angry often;

sometimes they go without speaking; they just let things blow over until they've put the argument behind them.

Verbal fights make matters worse: S/O are best friends who can turn into the worst of enemies; S/O have endured many violent fights, both physically and emotionally abusive, with inconsiderate, selfish feelings, and harsh criticism over nearly everything, just to make the other feel bad; they can say awful things without actually realizing the actual degree of hurt that is caused, and then pretend that nothing has happened. S/O fight about anything and everything; they thrive on conflict—they're so afraid of being cut off that they try to cram lots of stuff into a short period—in the end no one's mind is changed, and they both end up very frustrated.

S/O were roommates who shared food together; one day S noticed that someone had used her stir-fry sauce—O was the only one who had rice for supper, so the next day S bluntly told O that she owed her a bottle of sauce and it turned into a psycho—blown up fight—the fight was over something so small and dumb, but this sauce, at the same time, was sacred in their apartment; soon O turned cold and irrationally moved out—it seemed to build on both sides and suddenly blew up all at once.

S/O could have fought World War III because they have such an adversarial style of interaction that always had to have a winner; S worked hard to avoid that type of interaction, but O seemed to thrive on it, subjecting everyone else to sharp condescension—finally S had enough and joined the battle with relish; they looked for each other's vulnerabilities and exploited them—points of possible agreement were dismissed as useless; twisting each other's words became an art form— big points were to be gained from this tactic; taking offense at innocuous comments was an excuse to start another fight; being right was critical—even defending a position O know was ridiculous to admit she was wrong. S/O have fights and problems, but they have a hard time facing and confronting conflict; they don't like to deal with conflict in the same way; O does not like to fight and wants to be left alone, while S likes to fight in order to face it and get it over with—this makes it very hard for S/O to get their feelings out in the open. S/O can say anything, but unless they are careful and censor what they say, a fight follows and there is very any winner—it is amazing they have not killed each other; they try to reason with the other, but it never helps—they try to understand the other's viewpoint, but it's hard; they yell, roll their eyes, or make snide comments about what the other says, all of which evolves into an argument on lots of touchy subjects.

Hurtful outcomes: S/O say awful, abusive things that are easy to be hurt by. S/O do not want to face the truth of how much O has hurt S. S/O talk, while S thinks O thrives on hurting others. S/O avoid the topic of X because O's opinion hurts S very much. S/O find that S gets hurt feelings when O doesn't call S on the phone. S/O got along well at first, but although S still finds O's life interesting, O never felt likewise for S, who felt very hurt and defeated. S/O often let off steam about what they don't like about each other, and these things end up hurting each other's feelings and make the apartment tense and unbearable. S/O talk, but S finds herself getting annoyed at things O says—S replies with short answers, or she doesn't say a lot, and S can tell that O feels hurt by this treatment—S feels guilty, and she makes an extra effort to be nice to O for a while, but sooner or later it starts all over again. S/O have disagreements where S thinks O seems not to have a feel for when enough is enough—O is self-righteous and will keep antagonizing just to make herself feel better—this leads to hurt feelings and some grudges held into the future. S/O are two different people who each want to convince the other to see things differently, but this doesn't work, and all that results is more trouble because someone gets hurt or one person compromises or gives up to avoid further disputes.

Strong signs of negativity are a leading indicator of a strong disposition to discredit or devalue others in an insensitive, abusive, or senseless manner. Intense negativity, when taken personally, is painful to endure in large doses. It hurts, after all, to be chronically subject to relentless or unrelieved censorship, criticism, castigation, or condemnation before other people. Boundary violations of core values are vulnerable.

If respect, honesty, and trust are cherished values, they cannot be undermined without an implied sense that integrity of the person is under attack. Valued subjects are the very ones that give life endurable meaning and affirmative validation. Core values must be defended and protected from external disruption and turmoil. Patience and tolerance are likely to be sorely tested when boundary violations intensify without relief or restoration.

A wide spectrum of troubling disputes and dense entanglements have potential to unfold, sometimes, without cause or reason. With no end in sight. Strong advocates are likely to be wrapped up in complex difficulties or problematic matters. Suddenly, they are at risk for greater entrapment in misdirected or misguided exchange relations. Protracted difficulties are likely to multiply in unfavorable, unstable, or unsettled social transactions.

Sometimes what starts out as a simple point of disagreement may well end up as being nothing more than a single point of minor dispute. At other times, what starts out as a single point of disagreement may lead into a complex of deeply embedded issues and a blunt forewarning of things to come. Serious disagreements, none the less, give rise to questions, puzzles, and contradictions that are not easy to resolve, much less decipher. Moreover, unresolved stress and tension is difficult to decode or disentangle, particularly when key issues are badly conflated or unduly constrained in a maze of unspoken differences that go unstated or undetected in a mindless manner.

Avoidance occurs when rivals lack the ability or willingness to subject implicit, unspoken tensions to explicit forms of recognition. What is left out of deliberation can matter a great deal to someone who cannot find a way to express what seems inexplicable. A feeling of futility may follow from a disoriented sense of fault or failure to find the right words or know how to restore a neutral style that is no longer abusive or intolerant.

Regressive styles often serve to shift a mess of toxic disagreements backward and, thereby, threaten to magnify the scope, scale, or significance of unfinished business. Past issues can be recalled, one after another, in a maze of name calling, as a distractive device. Aggressive fighters know how deflect attention away from a critical subject, simply as a tactical advantage. Instead, change the topic, pile, on, distract, confuse, or assign fault and failure. Protracted disputes appear to move in and out of varying states, degrees, or gradations of difficulty and perplexity without end in sight.

When serious disputes turn into irreconcilable differences, it may be virtually impossible to unpack them one by one. Sticky situations prevail where one advocate attempts to confront what another advocate tries to conceal. The tension between 'uncovering' and 'covering' up can be prolonged indefinitely. It may get to the point where there is less and less to say about more and more about thick disputes than ever before. Difficulties multiply when simple points of discord congeal together and multiply in spirals of escalation with no way to stop. In the emotional aftermath, agitated parties may withdraw, go for long periods of time without talking, without so much as a single word or gesture. Touchy subjects are absorbed or internalized, in protracted states of mutual silence. When words and gestures stop working, there may be no way to know how to make them work again, without access to corrective devices. Denial and refusal go together in a linguistic vacuum. One person hints at a desire to bring up an innocuous topic only to have another deny its relevance in a curt dismissal.

Another passive tactic invites refusal to admit to the sheer magnitude of what has gone wrong. Some defensive advocates hide true feelings and make others think that they share the same views, when in fact they do not. Others defend inert tendencies, through acts of delay, deferral, or denial in which their words, thoughts, and deeds are inconsistent but in which implicit, tacit contradictions go unnoticed.

Living in a state of denial involves minimal engagement in public acts without focus or awareness under conditions in which focus and awareness should be taken as given, as obvious. Hence, denial rules out whenever one refuses to accept or confront what takes place. Acts of inattention and deflection promote passivity, avoidance, and disavowal of real-life evens for purposes of disowning unwanted features of self-presentation by distorting manipulative meanings in public conflicts. A more active tactic occurs when one shifts focus by a denial of what another has to say. Discredit of opposing appeals can go on indefinitely, until one or more give up a game without end.

Weak arguments are useful devices in human encounters. They function as signs of caution. Change direction. Struggle for options. Explore alternatives. Brief disputes are tolerated. They prevent conflated faith that intractable agreements will soon rule the day. Tensions between agreement and disagreement give cause and reason to sort them out and find a better way. Personal adaptation and mutual accommodation may give rise to greater awareness that explicit differences between rivals can mean that they both are right in their own way. Strong differences lose some of their sting when they yield to compromise and moderation. Negative disaffection test resolve to defend and justify strong affection (as suitable replacements).

The desire for intense disputes is undermined by those who feel inferior, inadequate, or insufficient in the defense of their ethical or moral standards. There is not much residual value in the perpetuation of unresolved matters that destroy attachments and drive (previously) congenial partners apart. Verbal fights employ words and gestures as symbolic weapons to cause hurt and harm. Relational alliances dissolve when injured parties walk away in despair.

Mutual Understanding

S/O respond well to shifting changes from day to day. They share a similar range of moods quite often: joy, happiness, laughter, sadness, anger, and calm. They know how to act when one feels one way and the other feels another. Both try hard to alleviate bad moods by leaving friendly notes, treats in the fridge, or cards on the desk. Usually S knows when to leave O alone, when O is in a mood to get picked on, or needs support. It is a result of making the effort plus natural rapport. Rarely do they get upset with one another. Comment accent: having fun, play backgammon, studying, listening to music, or going out for a drink; it takes time and effort to achieve a spirit of genuine care and concern.

S/O have been together for a long time and know each other very well. Each one has a deep understanding of what is important to the other. S knows O better than anyone else and O knows S better too. They share things never said or told to anyone else, and both show sides of themselves that others never see. S/O know how to identify feelings and moods and they appreciate and respect one another's beliefs and attitudes. Each one has acquired a deep appreciation for the unique contributions of the other.

S/O enjoy one another, joke a good deal, pick up on quicks, and use a lot of sarcasm. They like to laugh and say things that cause more laughter. It isn't picking on each other, they just say things that aren't true but it would be funny if they were. It's hard to explain what transpires, but they don't take it all apart and see what it means. S/O state their positions, make comments, ask questions, but without big discussion of any issue. The quality of interaction is high because both know how to response to what the other needs.

S/O interact well together. They do not let problems stand in the way for very long. It is not necessary to spell everything out in verbal terms; there is an unspoken knowledge of the other. When O walks into the room, S knows right away whether O is stressed, upset, happy, tired, and so on, and vice versa. Both know when to have a good time to talk and when it is better to leave one another alone. S/O know how hard to push for information and when to back off; they know what secrets can be told to others and which ones must be kept confidential. The list goes on. They can tell each other things neither one could ever tell to anyone else. They can laugh at things no one else would find remotely funny. There is shared resolve to maintain high levels of mutual understanding.

S/O are comfortable sharing personal feelings with one another. Neither one is afraid to say whatever comes to mind because each one knows the other will understand. Sometimes S or O will sense what the other is feeling before the other does. There is comfort where talk flows smoothly, except where each one starts to talk at the same time. Because each one can sense the other's frame of reference, it is easy to talk about personal problems. Such skills foster a strong level of mutual bond.

S/O have lived together for several years. Through effort, O knows what situations make O happy, sad, agitated, or irritated and how to deal with difficult times. S has learned how to identify similar feelings and reactions on S's part. They are very open and work hard at looking at complex issues from the other's point of view. Both avoid judgment and condemnation and rely instead on honesty and trust. When one acts in a hostile, irrational, or irritating manner, the chances are good that the other will be able to understand why, provide comfort, and diffuse tension by talking through touchy feelings and sensitive concerns.

S/O discuss worries, problems, dreams, futures, and relations with others. S/O share agreement and understanding of each other's difficulties. They discus personal issues in detail. Topics of discussion include money, friendship, and future questions. S/O view the world in the same way. They know each other best so they are able to be completely open and honest. S/O call each other every day with nothing in particular to say because it seems weird not to talk. S/O share the same value system and that is probably why there is such a high level of mutual understanding. They respond with a lot of feedback because they want to understand each other better rather than be content to pick a fight.

S/O feel refreshed, renewed, and inspired every time they interact with each other. Their interactions are so simple, yet so complete. S/O are comfortable in each other so no tension is involved. S/O poste important questions. They are confident in the other's ability to listen wholeheartedly and respond empathetically. S/O are never insecure when talking because they both know that no matter how shocked, taken aback, perturbed, confused, intrigued, bored, or elated the other maybe, they can sense the passion even when they don't fully understand. Mutual trust is built on healthy relations in times of need or routine conditions as well. It is so easy to be with each other, so basic, so uncomplicated.

S/O have been together for nearly two years. They have grown to understand each other well. When S/O discuss important matters, they try hard to listen first, respond next, and come to come type of compromise. If they have a disagreement about something, they decide whether or not it warrants discussion. If it does, they try to find a time to sit down with an implicit understanding that they will discuss it until something gets accomplished. It may be what hurts, what made them mad, why they reacted the way they did, and so on. If they see a way to resolve the problem, and not let it occur again, they promise to employ a useful method of resolution. Open discussion of different views leads to a better understanding of each other. S/O have come to accept each other for who they are and how they express themselves. Mutual love has allowed them to adapt a unique method and most of the time they meet in the middle and leave each one satisfied with the outcome.

S/O are friends who just seem to agree easily and without much hassle. The main reasons is listening. When O talks, S really listens. S doesn't just hear O, but tries to see the deeper meaning behind O's words. O does the same thing when S talks. They agree so well because they try to understand what the other is really saying. S/O respect each other enough not to disregard each other's thoughts and feelings. It doesn't hurt that they have the same values and morals as a base to start each conversation that leads to such strong levels of mutual understanding.

S/O talk about things they have in common. Conversations just seem to flow very well. They don't have to explain or justify their feelings. S/O express themselves openly and honestly. They are not afraid to tell each other their true reactions—there is no holding back. S/O have so many common assumptions and similar interest they can presume, rightly so, the other will agree about what is said or done. They treat each other with mutual respect. S/O let each other finish their thoughts when they speak and neither interrupts, and that makes it easier to understand. S/O often refer to troubling things in their lives and they try to offer solutions. They respect each other's decisions and let one another know how much they value their friendship.

S/O are close friends. When they talk, there is a lot of trust. S/O discuss a variety of things ranging from sex, friends, school, and family. They laugh and cry together. S/O console and support each other. They have gone through similar experiences and have similar beliefs. S/O conduct themselves in similar ways, have mutual respect, which enables them to listen and understand. They trust each other's opinions and they feel free to ask for advice. S/O look at the world in the same way, tell each other anything, even silly ones. They make each other laugh or be serious too. S/O are very clear and articulate about any topic of discussion. They are firm in their positions and on important matters but are unable to waver. S/O love to spend time together. They react in a rationale, conservative, loving, and respectful manner. They will be life-long friends.

S/O have the easiest time talking because they understand each other the best. They agree about what each other may say or do. The feeling is a mutual source of comfort. S/O can discuss virtually anything. Because they share such strong agreement, they can have deep, serious talks about life, people, and feelings. These talks occur on a regular basis. No matter what causes them to agree, they like having a close friend to share beliefs, values, and interests. It makes them feel sure of themselves.

S/O are attuned to what transpires in their daily lives. They discuss whatever problems arise in the course of the day. S/O attempt to be very honest with each other. S/O understand that lying is not the answer. If they do disagree, they are quick to let it be known right away. S/O do not avoid conflict or let hostilities brew. Friendship is important. It's strange how their goals and interests are the same. Each one wants something special out of life and has a plan to acquire major goals. They believe in the same laws of life and reinforce these beliefs whenever one begins to slip. S/O have a true friendship with no hidden urges or ulterior motives.

Empathy matters: S/O like to cheer each other up and bring a smile when the other's having a bad day. S/O like to tell each other everything that is going on in the course of their lives. S/O like to talk about absolutely anything—they are comfortable with each other; they are very much alike and they react to things similarly. S/O like to watch tv, drink, gamble, play video games, talk about work, dating women—they understand every statement, even about difficult topics. S/O like the same things and they can talk about almost anything; this ability to discuss anything (no matter what) promotes a greater level of mutual understanding. S/O like to explain things, and that helps both express themselves or rephrase something one didn't mean and wants to take back. S/O have mutual understanding that transcends verbal interaction. S/O express their true feelings without being indirect—they express themselves clearly, honestly—mutual understanding is based on honesty, trust, genuine, clear, and true expressions of desire, positive encouragement and true regard for one another. S/O share deep understanding that goes beyond a typical relationship— both would be willing to do anything for the other; it goes without saying.

Love matters: S/O have shared tough times together; sometimes they have fought like cats and dogs, but when all is said and done, S/O have the ability to share their lives and understand each other so well; they see wonderful things in each other, due to a deep sense of unconditional love; they are able to say negative or hurtful things and still discover a renewed sense of mutual understanding—no matter what; they find a way to relate to one another's perspective; knowing deep down that they understand each other so ell is what makes a big difference in their lives. S/O have a deep love which means they strive to maintain harmony; both assume the best of intentions and must be given all the chance in the world to clarify, before jumping to conclusions—the outcome is a feeling of warmth and comfort. S/O understand each other very well; they share the same moods: joy, happiness humor; whether sad, angry, calm. S/O coexist—what it takes most is genuine care and friendly love for one another.

Care matters: S/O care deeply for each other; they are considerate of each other's feelings and adjust quickly to accommodate each other's needs; they feel comfortable and don't need to put up a front; they are able to express a wide range of emotions and know what to expect and count on each other in times of need. S/O engage in a great deal of give-and-take; they express themselves freely without getting defensive; it is given that they really trust each other's judgment; they are so comfortable that they can say virtually anything; because they respect each other's advice, they don't take criticism personally or negatively; there is a great amount of care that goes on; no one attacks the other, and they take into account how what they say will affect the other. S/O know their words and gestures will always go together; they discuss feelings openly and without ridicule; they talk about personal issues, receive support an encouragement; they treat each other with respect and dignity at all times; they express real feelings without being indirect or pretend, they are honest and express themselves clearly. S/O are different but the magnitude of difference actually brings them together; they rarely fight, because they know each other so well—not to mention that S has known O since birth, so S has seen O through it all and knows O inside out, which makes it all the more easy to understand; they express their true selves and hold nothing back; whether they agree or disagree, they still understand each other's moods and when to leave things alone; they listen deeply and treasure advice; when they go out and things get messed up or go wrong, it's no big deal because they both know they really care about one another—their friendship will endure because through good times and bad times they manage to understand how each one thinks and feels.

S/O get along great, think alike, enjoy similar things; they connect on the same level; they talk on the phone and visit each other, but no matter how much times has passed, they always catch up quickly; they enjoy each other's company, understand what the other is saying, care greatly, and remain very close; they are the best friends in the world; they rarely get into disputes; they have a deep understanding of each other—they do not know what they would do without each other. S/O come to a mutual understanding by compromising; there is mutual give-and-take; they talk, listen, and do not interrupt until the other is finished—strong understanding helps them think and learn from the other; mutual understanding helps them settle differences in a respectful manner; they know how to comfort each other; when there is something wrong; they know what and how the other thinks and feels, and they can reflect on one another's feelings; they care about how the other feels, and they don't say anything that will make the other upset; interactions involve a lot of love, care, and understanding; they talk mainly about things in their daily lives; they do almost everything together.

Enjoyment matters: S/O enjoy daily talks because each one strives to promote the highest level of mutual understanding possible. S/O enjoy talking a lot—they'll go on forever. S/O are there to console and make the other feel better—a lot of time is spent just talking and enjoying each other's company; S/O talk about their futures, plans in life, lack of plans, current relations, past relations, families and their effects; sometimes they talk about nothing and instead just spend time walking the dog in the woods; they seem to enjoy these times as much as those spent in deep conversation. S/O can enjoy almost any social activity together; both believe what the other is saying is true— that kind of confidence and support goes a long way in this world; knowing they understand each other makes a big difference in their lives. S/O lead common lifestyles, enjoy the same things, and look to each other and understand whatever is said or done. S/O enjoy each other's company— they have a common understanding of each other, but they never know what to expect next—they get along better because of this—they look at each other in amazement about all that has happened in the short time they have known each other—when they talk, they don't say much.

Human encounters give rise to a duel task: to understand each other well and minimize risk of misunderstanding. Struggle is magnified in complex or confusing disputes in which it appears that little or nothing can be done to make common sense of what transpires. In effect, the pursuit of understanding implies the risk of misunderstanding. No other type of empirically verified conception is worthy of consideration. Misguided beliefs lead all too easily to the false conviction that the ideas we signify by our words and gestures are, coincidently, the same as others, as signified by the use of those same words and gestures.

The concept of understanding is elusive. What it means to achieve a state of genuine understanding with other people is not easily settled. Not surprisingly, it turns out that there are as many viable ways to define the larger question as there are alternative ways to search for satisfactory answers. The central construct is an old-fashioned notion that simply cannot stand alone, much less as disembodied from real-life conditions.

As initial presumption, it is useful to think of human understanding as an unfinished work in progress. Comprehension remans incomplete or partial; the process is complete only when there is closure. During daily events we are immersed in provisional states of understanding that are not complete until the day is over. Only in a retrospective glance are we capable or know not only what has taken place but also how it ended up. Hence, tentative states of understanding occur prior to a state of being fully understood. Mutual achievements are potentially infinite and inexhaustible rather than fixed or final, without sufficient opportunity for revision or reinterpretation. Salient conditions are also subject to endless revaluation and cross-checking, as bounded by tradition, social context, and fashioned form irregular or cyclical movements rather than a liner process or bold step from ignorance to truth.

The difference between understanding (incomplete) in the presence tense and having been understood (complete) matters because it permits social agents to take advantage of incomplete activity and correct errors and mistakes before a state of culmination is obtained. Likewise, tentative misunderstanding can be relocated when they occur rather than later when they are over and the full impact is complete. Practical application: act a certain way and tentative understandings are likely to prevail over complete misunderstanding. The point is to recognize the difference, minimize damage, and take corrective action while there is still time.

Working agreement and mutual understanding are not exclusive categories. It is virtually impossible for even the most articulate social agents to engage in unconditional agreements without also producing conditional disagreements at the same time. the same principle holds for the ratio of understanding and misunderstanding. There is a critical difference in the distribution of these major categories. It is easy to identify expressed agreements because they are largely observable, verified, and explicit. It is harder to identify working disagreements for three main reasons. One, socially undesirable features of exchange relations have less currency and credit, they are susceptible, therefore, to denial or cover-up. Agreements are achievements. Two, socially undesirable aspects of disagreement may go undetected by one party who hides them from inspection while the other may be oblivious to another's sense of misalignment. Three, it may be more difficult to translate implicit disagreement into explicit form.

Multiple meanings work well together: responses are predictable; talk is expansive; topics move from surface to depth; reciprocity rewards acceptance; comfort is high; discomfort is low; acceptance prevails over rejection; advocates know what to say or do; support multiplies; help is always on the way; core values protect; competence leads to compatibility; meaning systems match up; common ground feels precious and delicate; inevitable differences do not last long; there is enough time to know where everyone stands; stay open, honest, receptive; agreement displaces disagreement; conversations flow easily; frictions do not last a long time Explanations are hard to find. It is not clear what capacities, abilities, and skills must be activated for working agreement and mutual understanding to converge into coherent form. It is one thing to keep track of what is collectively achieved. It is quite another to identify what makes collective achievements register in such striking form.

Collective Misunderstanding

S/O fail to grasp intentions, values, and ideas as a matter of course. The severity of misunderstanding allows no room to step back and gain a better picture of what transpires. Preexisting frames of reference are automatically imposed on every little thing. One party will offer a response that fails to put oneself n the other's shoes or to account for why the other feels a certain way. Daily contacts are largely limited to surface agreement but still ignore larger, underlying questions because of the pervasiveness of unresolved misunderstandings that stand in the way.

S/O don't let "meanings" sink in. Each one is quite good at giving up when sick and tired of fighting and too stubborn to hear the other's view. Usually fights end up in a fiasco of yelling followed by not interaction for days on end. They don't let each speak their pieces due to a matter of one-perspective goals. Often S will find herself regressing more and more into O's view of "my way or the highway." Often S is the only one who wishes for change. Every year it gets harder and harder to understand one another. S/O have drifted apart and now live separate lives. It is more difficult to know the other's intentions. When they do fight, it is so easy to throw put-downs, which only produce more arguments. Finally, S/O never talk about problems at hand. They are sure to move off the subject, even to the point where neither one realizes why they began fighting in the first place.

S/O would be more understanding if only they did not disagree over so many little things along the way. S knows that O misconstrues S's intentions. S will pay O a complement and O will think that S is being sarcastic just to annoy O. At times, they do it to each other. When S tries to apologize for acting in a certain way, O interprets O's actions as antagonizing O even more. S feels some of the ideas going through O's head are simply wrong. If S could understand why O believes a certain way, S would more likely agree with O's viewpoint. Mutual misunderstanding is a huge and overwhelming obstacle to overcome.

S/O have had a lot of misunderstandings lately. S was brought up in a family that didn't promote a lot of direct exchange and so S does not know the rules of everyday conversation. S says things that make O mad and this makes S even more mad. The other morning, after O was curling her hair, O asked S whether S wanted the curling iron left on. S said "no" as if O had asked if S could burn o with it. Deep down, S knows O didn't mean it, but it still makes S furious. Eventually S stopped talking to O because O did not like to be treated this way. This went on for a while before they finally broke the barrier and not everything is back to normal. If S/O could understand how the other feels, things would improve and misunderstanding would be a thing of the past.

S/O drive one another crazy. Simple body language provides a strong indication of mutual intolerance. Due to different styles and outlooks on virtually everything, routine contacts are plagued with constant disputes and endless misunderstandings. Comments direct at S, or others, that O views to be harmless, S views as inconsiderate and hurtful. Sarcastic comments that S throws out to lighten the tension only end up irritating O even more. Also, O misreads S's actions while staying on the defensive. Most direct exchanges are guarded, adversarial, and combative. S/O refuse to open up and take down the walls that have been erected to protect themselves. There is nothing more frustrating than to try to interact in a friendly and effective manner only to end up in an impasse. Recently, S/O have not even bothered to tray. Constructive criticism is blown out of proportion and taken as a personal attack by one or both parties. Small talk is analyzed again and again to find some hidden insult or discredit. Incompatible styles of self-presentation and discordant viewpoints produce disastrous failures. After such unfulfilling, frustrating encounters, S/O have decided to give up and settle instead for a state of perpetual confusion and misunderstanding.

S/O once engaged in a great deal of direct contact in the past. Recently, however, due to persistent misunderstandings, they have begun to avoid each other. O goes on and on, talking about basic information in a highly elaborated stream of opinion and speculation. Lots of other topics are sprinkled in. S cannot follow abstract thought processes that O puts into words without editing or refinement. Sometimes when O is talking, S nods in agreement only to find out five minutes later that S had an entirely wrong idea about what O was trying to express. They must have incompatible styles. S doesn't think O would be where O is today if everyone else felt as consumed a S does. S feels uneasy talking with O who seems to misinterpret S's remarks and get the wrong idea entirely. Sometimes O acts as though S has offended O with some other intended meaning, hint, or implication.

S/O do not get along well. There is considerable misunderstanding, but they never discuss what matters most. S doesn't understand what O wants in in response to O's millions of comments. Shas to listen to O talk to other friends to make sense of what O is saying. S tries to joke with O as with other friends, but O still doesn't respond well. They have drifted into a passive relationship. S/O rarely sit down and talk. Brief conversations revolve around trivial comments. S thinks about the deeper implications of not being able to get along and not know how or what to say or do.

S/O disagree a lot. S is serious, quiet, and reserved, while O is loud, rowdy, and sarcastic. Conversations are skewed because neither one knows how to interpret sensitive feelings of the other. S dismisses much of what O says as sarcastic. As a result, S is irritated, defensive, and no longer opens up out of fear of a sarcastic response. In a sense, D has become gun-shy. Biggest problems arise when O does try to be sincere and doesn't intend to create difficulties. S/O stay as friends but are still quite anxious. Because S expects the worst, S is overly sensitive to O's comments and remains on the defensive because of the inability to tell the difference between O's sincerity and sarcasm.

S/O live together but rarely see each other anymore. This makes a simple task appear to be imposing. When they do talk, one will get the wrong meaning of what was said. S avoids O, who gets defensive and takes things the wrong way. S can also tell how O feels about things because O doesn't voice deep feelings or show much emotion. The solution to so many misunderstandings has been to just let them pass. This hasn't been effective, however, as it produces very negative feelings as a result. S thinks O bottles things up more than O used to. Because O is not around much, O doesn't understand S or what S means to say. The same holds the other way.

Anger makes matter worse: S/O are often stern, strict, angry, bitter, upset. S/O find it hard to determine if either one hurt or angry. S/O belittle, jump all over one another and down each other's throats over trivial and unimportant things—the result is anger, frustration, and mutual contention. S/O used to get so angry that now they don't want to talk about it anymore. S/O nag, talk gets heated, and they often end up in a screaming match involving everything they don't like about each other, they stay angry for a day or two. S/O clash—they want what's best for each other, but they never get to the point of showing it; they hate fighting and pain but they can't get past it; the saddest part is knowing that so much anger and pain can stem from overpowering love, which itself is frightening and sickening—they fall into the same degraded patterns every time they see each other. S/O find it is rare that either party has a clue as to what the other party is talking about—one yells, screams, and gets angry while the other party (laid back) reacts with confusion—this only causes more anger; every time the talk, they fight. S/O don't always know whether the other is playing around or acting seriously. This often leads to severe arguments which are then later disregarded by both of them. S/O have serious misunderstandings; they don't always state what they want clearly, but each one still expects the other to grasp what is being said anyway; when each one gets angry about what the other misunderstood, they start to be sarcastic and find that sarcasm conveys hostility and anger but it doesn't really get the message across; it also makes the other defensive or unwilling to listen; each one expects the other to understand just from nonverbal cues what the other is feeling—such as slamming things around, turning the music up, or ignoring one another. S/O do not understand each other; they don't talk about anything that matters; they don't know how to be open with each other so they just end up not knowing how the other thinks or feels at all.

Productive use of ordinary language cannot be isolated from adverse effects of misuse or abuse of common idioms. In difficult situations, with tension between effective and ineffective adaptation, misuse of words and gestures are signs of inability or unwillingness to knowhow to talk, what to say, or take corrective action. If it takes ability and skill to avoid mutual misunderstanding, it must take even more ability and skill to know what to do when things go wrong. Personal awareness of defective and deficient use of words and gestures need not be cause or reason to give up hope in locating a better vocabulary as a literacy measure.

Usual, unexpected, or uncertain public disputes magnify complexity and complication of intentional choice and unintended outcomes. Touchy problems multiply, one after another, without an equal number of viable solutions in sight.

Whereas mutual disagreements are often simply self-evident, entangled misunderstandings may operate well below the surface of conscious awareness and beyond anyone's corrective grasp.

Serious misinterpretations, as a rule, typically extend well beyond the scope or scale of simple disagreements; the same holds true for the heavy burdens of collective misunderstanding. Where explicit agreements or multiple understandings are in short supply, routine acts of misinterpretation, miscommunication, and misunderstanding may proliferate in the absence of applied social knowledge as a corrective mechanism. Problematic conditions may well reflect a surplus of surface disagreements, deep-seated misunderstandings, of an uneven combination of linguistic confusion.

Failure to grasp of comprehend direct modes of social negotiation are likely to lead to massive layers of collective misunderstanding that differ in significance from mistakes, miscalculations, or misguided or misdirected application of practical logic or informed reasoning. Escalations of serial arguments and proliferating misunderstandings are serious impediments to personal identity, social interaction, collective knowledge, or cultural solidarity.

In extreme cases, struggling parties may not know where to begin, how to proceed. What to do, or how to settle things down. Serious misunderstandings may resist corrective scanning. However, large-scale multiplication of chronic misunderstanding that penetrate small-scale operations may acquire added density and thereby resist all efforts to make things better up and down the line.

What causes the greatest amount of collateral damage will entail subversive interplay between small-scale misunderstanding (speech acts) and large-scale divisions stemming from repeated failure to recognize ethnic diversity or cultural variation. In the final analysis, transactional failures cannot be reduced to discrete matters of identity, style, status, or rank but rather to the fragile and precarious aspects of the entire system itself.

Leading themes: intentions, plans, and goals interfere; overwhelming obstacles ae difficult to overcome; failures are hurtful; criticism is blown out of proportion; hidden insults are common; avoidance is defensive; styles are incompatible; some do not know what to say to do to make things right; meanings are twisted beyond measure; personal defects multiply without end; no way to get past pain, frustration, anger; just walk away and out the door.

In sum, human attachments are not secured in the absence of meaning systems, convergent influences, and wide latitudes of collective understanding. Periodic outbreaks of disagreement and misunderstanding are intrinsic features of daily life. It is not necessary to wish them away but rather keep them at bay. A life worth living requires far more than power, affection, and engagement in worthy projects. Mortal existence invites struggle to treat others the way we would want them to treat ourselves. Lived experience is not only additive but subtractive as well. Little things mean a lot. Everything matters, what is kept and what is thrown away.

The liberating power of words and gestures are not incidental factors in the larger scheme of things. It pays to know the difference between use, misuse, and abuse. The same pragmatic rule holds for the magnitude of difference between interpretation and misinterpretation, agreement and disagreement, understanding and misunderstanding. Productive meaning systems are not locked up inside some dark, interior chamber. The best way forward is to construct viable projects that can withstand the regressive pressures of incompetence, incompatibility, and incongruity.

Summary

Human attachments are not risk free. Systemic exploitation and protracted oppression render strong bonds useless. Avoidance of coercive attachments permits escape from tedium and drudgery. Impersonal exchanges occur in anonymous public settings where neither a strong bond of resilient meanings is necessary for routine outcomes. Strong bonds are required where human attachments are welcome or desired. Weak bonds are not displaced in risk-reward calculations. Secure attachments align with favorable conditions, affirmative activities, and collective knowledge. Labor-intensive effort is needed to protect safe and secure investments as distinctive achievements. Conjunctive influences bring striving subjects together; disjunctive factors drive them apart. Working agreements are an indispensable means to produce broad latitudes of expansive meaning systems. Ultimate valuations are at stake. Daily conversations reinforce interest, pleasure, and enjoyment of being together. Good stuff multiplies, even if bad stuff does not go away. An abiding spirit of mutuality facilitates a deliberate search for common ground. Surface disclosures lead to deeper truth. Agreeableness qualifies as a stable personality trait that counteracts argumentativeness.

Working disagreements move in the opposite direction, away from productive engagement and toward regressive setbacks. Negative disaffection is difficult to tolerate in large doses. In general, the negative effects of protracted disagreement are far more salient, intense, and lasing that the positive effects of their affirmative counterparts. A prior surplus of constructive alignments can be squandered and dissolve in downward spirals. Verbal fights make matters worse. Harmful outcomes spin out of control. Discredit and devaluation are common maladies. Intense pain leads some discouraged advocates to resort to avoidance, distance, detachment, or desire to walk away.

Conversely, working agreement and mutual understanding are moderately correlated. Shared agreements rely heavily on verbal cues and benign attributions. Mutual understanding, in contrast, involve greater sensitivity to nonverbal cues. Surface presumption of shared understanding is likely to prevail in the absence of visible signs of confusion, ambivalence, and ambiguity. It is easy to assume because we agree that we also understand but verified agreement is no assurance that mutual understanding is taking place at the same time. Constructive expressions of love, care, and enjoyment are derived benefits. Protracted misunderstanding is likely to foster negative signs: anger, impatience, frustration. Recovery of meanings systems requires resolute struggle to minimize the intrusion of incompetence and incompatibility from shared lexicons.

7

Subversive Influences

Human existence involves struggle against duress. Massive forces are imposed on all manner of living beings, up to outer limit of uncertainty and unpredictability. Survival requires ability to overcome stress, strife, and strain in daily life. Mortal existence depends on steadfast resistance to physical forces that are not easily dispatched. Social struggles are far less lawful and more rule governed. Life forces penetrate all living creatures who are also forces of life themselves.

Survival is never friction-free. Boundaries of life and death are not exclusive, a single point of origin or destination. Only uncertainty and unpredictability prevail. Individuals share their biographical narratives within generations and across generations. Every mortal being is granted only temporary provision to be fully present in a world of creative inquiry. Living expectations are not reality tested at a fixed rate. Optimal conditions may preserve longevity expectations that it is possible to live a long life and also live well. The critical question: what makes life worth living. The search for a good life is an unfinished work in progress.

Human struggle implicates collective resolve to live with nature and nurture in a state of coexistence.

There are no fixed limits to a human life span. Odds of survival decline in middle and old age. Neither time nor space are free of constraints. Longevity does not stay unfettered. The future is never guaranteed. Nothing stays the same for very long. Only uncertainty, ambiguity, and indeterminacy prevail. What causes dying and death, without premature exposure to chronic illness, is slippage from power, strength, and control back to frail and fragile conditions of physical weakness and mental deterioration. Mortality accelerates, gathers momentum, salience, and intensity, then declines. Age diminishes ability to recover from inevitable toll of stress, strain, friction and strife.

Risk

The puzzle is to figure out what makes life worth living in the highest sense of the term. Requisite capacities, abilities, and skills are available to literate persons. The central aim is to maximize advantages and minimize disadvantages. Each person, regardless of innate ability or acquired skill, can determine what is feasible to achieve, as defined by personal standards of credible conduct. Strength gathers momentum through firm resolve to maximize the use of all affordable resources. Strength diminishes with failure to find purpose, meaning, and fulfillment in the daily grind. Some people get worn out from relentless force of friction, strife, and strain. Other people refuse to settle for compromises. Still others do whatever it takes to foster an abiding sense of ultimate purpose in goal-directed aims.

Everyone suffers because no one is immune. Pain is a feature or human existence. Friction, strife, and strain are the price to be paid for the option to live, survive, and die alongside others who are accorded the same fate. Literate devices are available to prolong life and postpone death. Everyone has to figure out how to make the most out of what is available to them. A modest goal is to strive for the best and avoid the worst of what mortal existence has to offer. It is not always feasible or plausible to know how to live the best way imaginable. Optimal conditions are not easily achieved or effortlessly sustained. What makes life go well is revealed in inspirational satisfactions that are worthy of a distinctive calling.

Mixed motives multiply. Supportive urges are designed to endure, sustain, withstand, or tolerate unrelenting pressures. Subversive urges are designed to overthrow dominate powers of prevailing practices. Support adds vigor and vitality to what subversive factors dilute or degrade the pursuit of worthy projects. Support aligns with security. Subversion aligns with insecurity. Preservation of safety and security hangs in the balance. These mixed motives are not polar opposites. Supportive alignments of majority interests may be imposed on minority interests in an oppressive manner. Likewise, subversive activities gain traction as a means to galvanize resistance, rebellion, or protect against overwhelming authoritarian pressures. Risk assessments are critical priorities.

Risk involves chance, possibility of fortune or misfortune. Risky choices are unclear and uncertain. Little or nothing can be calculated well in advance. The past dissolves, the future impedes. Dumb luck is ruled out. Coincidence does not count. Gambling with hazards implies long odds. Nothing ventured, nothing gained. When everything is ventured (recklessly), nothing will be gained either way. Careless gambles with life, liberty, and freedom are the worst bet of all.

Careless gambling is a case in point. Not just money but living relations are put on the line. All-or-nothing bets are foolish, if not in the short-term, surely in the long-term. In a huge hall of dazzling lights, loud bells, and free drinks, only one happy winner will leave all the other unhappy losers behind. Casino owners know a secret, a magic spell. Entice chronic gamblers to stay long enough—impulsively, compulsively, foolishly—and one bitter truth intervenes. Owners use clever word magic to take all your chips away. On the way out the door, total losers are left to suffer despair. Dark corners of pawn shops, strip clubs, and loan sharks are available, for steep cost, to help pick up the slack. Nothing's left to do, except use chump change for a one-way ticket home, along with collateral damage, broken dreams, remorse, guilt, and shame.

Risky decisions are cast against probable results rather than absolute outcomes. Simple risks are taken one at a time. Complex risks expand in repeated trials. Pure avoidance of risk is never an option. Issues of gain and loss assume priority. Gains converge, unify, and multiply. Losses divide, separate, and distract. The margin of error shifts back and forth without fixed formula.

Physical settings impose their own assumptions on what social agents are able to make possible in daily life. Striving subjects must adapt, at all times, in all ways, to constraints and obstacles in habitable locations. Nothing is more upsetting than when the overwhelming force of nature renders or transforms a human community into unsettled, unstable form. Environmental disruption may well exceed what striving subjects can withstand.

The same hold true for life at the margins where toxic situations no longer permit constant access to clean air, water, nutrients, food, and subsistence needs. The protective cover of the ecological landscape must be preserved for human beings to grow and thrive in their natural world.

Physical forces and social influences do not simply dissolve into a massive collection of constraints and opportunities. The Earth is not just our home. It is a source of refuge, a shelter from cosmic storms. Earthly materials grant or deny access to human efforts to convert them into practical or useful form. Destruction of earthly territories implicates the destruction of life support systems just as well. Nature and nurture come together as a unified precondition for the reproduction of human species from one generation to another. Mantra: act out of respect for the lawful conditions of earthly surfaces or fall into doom and destruction.

Habitable settings remain stable and secure only if they can be settled and secured over time, depending on the physical and social pressures that evolve in chronic form. If human beings indulge in predatory destruction of other life forms, tolerate species' depletion, or justify willful disregard for conservation, then vital resources will degrade, and stable habitats will be placed in jeopardy. Coexistent valuations are necessary to protect human-wildlife interaction and interspecies contact. Abundant natural resources contribute to health, well-being, and labor-intensive projects. Collective thinking, emotional intelligence, empathy, and proactive initiatives work together to facilitate protection for viable life forms.

Social systems are vulnerable to degradation. Global networks, industrial expansion, elevated levels of production and consumption, all driven by rapid populations growth, are early warning signs of fragile and vulnerable cites of human habitation. Disrupted settlements magnify health risks. Local dislocations occur when occupied territories are irrevocably altered in destructive ways that foreclose or impede repair or restorative efforts. Uneven distribution of critical resources impedes the stability of social support networks.

Biodiversity is decisive. It drives the reproduction of shared activities that are needed to sustain the very core of life support systems. Windows of opportunity open up and close down. A vacated world is a symptom of moral failure. Every striving subject is granted an unspecified amount of time and space to explore a world of opportunity. Define, classify, explain, invest, care, and discover something that matters.

A meaningful way of life preserves the promise of fulfillment, one worth living, a higher purpose. Life signifies a capacity for growth, expansion, and self-regulation. Opportunity to explore what the world has to offer implicates the discovery of something to live for or against, rather than to linger for nothing at all. Life is everything. Death is nothing. Once life is over, it is absolutely over. Therefore, it is quite impossible to come back, and start all over again.

Ecological instability aggravates wasteful consumption of finite resources. An insatiable growth model presumes that the bearing capacity of the Earth can sustain population expansion virtually without limit. At a time when more and more people are struggling to compete for fewer and fewer resources, shrill demand for profits at all costs will surely prove very costly. Meanwhile, impoverished citizens are subject to moral exclusion from profit and prosperity. Their plight is easily forgotten, misplaced, or (re)located outside the civil boundaries of fair play

Where negative imperatives rule, fatal verdicts also prevail. No moral imperative to alleviate needless pain and suffering will make a decisive difference one way or another. It is odd. The growing gap between rich and poor gives rise to rationalization that refuses to redress grievance. Life-affirming values are necessary to promote unflinching regard for the sanctity of life, not just for the benefits of the rich and famous. All human beings are deserving of honor and dignity, unless proven otherwise. Striving subjects are entitled to make the most of their limited opportunities and prevent the worst from taking place.

A house is not a home. A temporary cite can provide relief from exhaustion, mobility, or migration. A tent, campsite, cabin, or motel will do just fine as a place to rest, sleep, and move on the next day. Safe and secure dwelling require far more. Stable human settlements require rational decisions to balance conflicting choices. Informed decisions are necessary to diminish ill health, particularly in densely populated urban areas. Ruined settlements are counteractive to principles of human stewardship. Sustainability requires a steady supply of material and energy to maintain efficiency and assimilate waste. Scarcity reduces collective capacity to satisfy needs, expectations and demands of a diverse population. Decreased energy reserves, climate change, and ecological degradation combine to make growth models difficult if not impossible to achieve. Only an aggressive fallacy assumes that infinite expansion can be sustained on a finite planet.

Loss of biodiversity implicates loss of aesthetic and artistic creativity in the face of impending crisis. However, restoration of intimate connections between human beings, wildlife, and nature reduces harmful effects of habitat loss. Improved conditions mitigate against climate change by enabling striving subjects to keep track of safe pathways and maintain evolutionary progress. Landscape diversity also provides a human community with aesthetic preferences and greater appreciation for the wonder of natural surroundings. Diverse typographies (air, sunlight, water, forest, river, stream) are linked to strong human engagements and pleasures derived from life sustained in beautiful settings. A strong sense of place has artistic value, along with historical and traditional artifacts, icons, and symbolic forms of representation. Fragmented settlements work in the opposite direction. Customs, habits, routines, and styles break down in disruptive contexts of diversity loss.

Natural desecration is not the only source of blame for willful neglect or destruction of human settlements. Disregard for life qualifies as a major factor in mortality risk. It is tragic to watch once stable and secure local neighborhoods deteriorate to the point of no return. Life is sacred only if it is cherished as the ultimate value. It is desecrated insofar as subversive devaluations are allowed to take its place. No one has yet come up with a convincing explanation for the ruthless plunder of once prosperous towns, cities, and regions of the United States. Millions of fragile and vulnerable citizens are forced to live in utter fear of their own lives. Terrified urban dwellers stay inside their locked doors and barricaded windows. Only a fool would dare walk down mean streets alone, unarmed, at night. Killing fields are no longer confined to military invasions. Collateral damage, civilians, count just as much. Sadly, ecological and humanitarian crisis are intimately connected.

Collective resilience depends on the capacity of human support systems to minimize constraints and maximize opportunities. Infrastructures are open to challenges from destabilizing impediments. Sustainable conditions increase global cooperation, diverse innovation, and open exchange of goods and services. Derived benefits promote economic prosperity, ecological restoration, and social mobility. Conversely, corrupting influences diminish the density and resilience of infrastructural integrity. Cascading failures follow from indecisive responses to critical issues. Cultural resilience requires public acknowledgment of diverse complications that impede progress. Problems multiply insofar as critical resources are unevenly distributed across local territories, cities, and states.

Urban blight is a symptom of ruthless destruction of vital human services. Broad sections of inner cities, dominated by gangs, drugs, and guns, are reduced to combat zones. Life is precarious for marginalized citizens who fear for their lives, homes, and schools. Anarchy and chaos rule where subversive factors have rendered once safe and secure neighborhoods unsafe and insecure. Terrified mothers hid their children in bathtubs to avoid the impact of stray bullets. Something is desperately wrong when innocent children are not granted safe passage back and forth to and from school. Home invasions are a way of life. Street violence goes unpunished where a no snitch rule enforces mandatory silence. Laws are rendered useless in the absence of equitable law enforcement. Money talks in a judicial system dominated by high priced lawyers who plea bargain violent felonies down to petty crimes. Three strike laws (you are out) fill up federal prisons at a rate that does not occur anywhere else in the developed world. Unfortunately, there are no algorithms to calculate the staggering waste of human potential, the number of lives cut short, of needless pain and suffering inflicted on those who have lost loved ones and now must bear unbearable burdens all by themselves.

Unstable sources of habitation, perhaps more than any other single factor, account for why so many troubled persons fail to achieve longevity or secure optimal quality of life. The cost of high-risk behavior is enormous. The margin of difference between health and illness is staggering. It is virtually impossible to calculate the true loss of potential linked to wasted years, shorter life spans or to what can never be reclaimed. Irreversible loss is irreversible, whatever the cause, whatever the reason, whatever the effect. Disabling risks say nothing of the misery and grief of those left behind.

Pain

Ordinary pain registers in brain tissue. Aversive pain results from multiple activation of brain circuits. A pain matrix is not a fixed state of activation but rather a fluid set of networks: inputs from salient recognition of bodily features of physical pain; intensity of noxious stimuli triggering broad cognitive (top-down) flow to insure pre-conscious transfers to conscious awareness. Pain occurs when receptors in nerve cells in the skin and internal organs detect potential damaging sensations. Intense painful feelings arise from bodily injury as well as injury to the mind. There is no pure physical or pure social pain but always a combination of the two.

Pain is processed in larger neural networks that partially overlap between conceptual and emotional arousal. There is considerable overlap in distressful events: physical pain activates an aversive state related to potential or actual potential injury or disease; social pain activates an aversive state of withdrawal from social exclusion, rejection, or ostracism; psychological pain activates an aversive state induced by incentive loss. Prolong exposure to social pain, with actual or potential damage to one's sense of social connection or social value, maybe processed by the same neural circuitry that processed physical pain. Shared neural circuitry contributes to physical and social pain overlap.

Pain is an adaptive mechanism and crude warning, either to attend to an injury or to avoid a potential source of further damage. Usually, an individual is able to take proper precautions, such as treating damaged parts of bodily tissue or escape from damage so the pain disappears rapidly. Therefore, in the short-term, physical pain serves as an escape alarm system. However, dur to complex interplay among physiological, phycological, and social factors, some painful conditions can compensate for acute pain—that is merely a symptom of injury—with chronic pain that constitutes a disease in itself. Protracted distress is one of the biggest health problems that can deeply impair personal ability to lead a satisfactory and productive life. The main functions of the pain system are not limited to signals of physical threat. Disruption of social relations trigger pain receptors in the brain. Social pain is defined as an unpleasant emotional response evoked by actual or potential separation from other social groups.

Brief pain episodes enable brain circuits to revert back to their normal state. Chronic, lasting pain, in contrast, leads to altered states that reduce shifts back to a normal baseline. Protracted pain alters the brain's response to potential threats. Repeated damage contributes to the transfer from acute, episodes of pain to chronic pain that lingers long after the effects of short-term pain have disappeared. Brief pain dissolves as soon as discomfort has been dealt with. However, over the course of repeated injuries, the brain's circuits reorganize, causing intense pain even when the original injury has been resolved.

Social and physical pain overlap in acute episodes and chronic conditions. Each one plays a role in the onset and control of both forms of pain in adverse ways that impair self-regulation and threats to basic psychological needs. Enduring socially painful events (e. g., being ostracized) could be as detrimental to survival as physical injury. A detection system may become overly sensitive to exclusions or rejection, thereby creating an alert system that leads to more false alarms.

Chronic pain can persist beyond healing time. It has, therefore, a major detrimental effect on quality of life and its negative impact on several aspects of personal well-being: loss of attachments, positive relations, and social adaptations. Chronic pain may persist, without any new physical injuries to provoke it. Repeated exposure to socially stressful events can alter sensitivity toward physical pain reactions. Where the system fails, repeated sensitization (from extreme vigilance) may not return to normal but result in lower pain thresholds, thereby creating a vicious cycle of hyper-detection of pain sensitivity. Chronic pain affects the whole person, invisibly, negativity, and adversely. It is not physical pain itself but rather the lasting outcomes of distress, loneliness, lost identity, and low quality of life. Pain of any kinds is notoriously difficult to express because it is often directly inaccessible and because it is not always linked to external objects.

Typical fear to pain levels are crucial to protecting a disaffected person from engaging in behavior that will result in bodily damage, but excessive fear of pain levels can increase a state of hypervigilance (external scanning) toward impeding pain-related stimuli. Selective attention to potential threats increases odds that actual or potential threats will be detected in conflated form. Toxic mix of acute distress and chronic pain are leading indicators of ostracism (being excluded or ignored). Combined threats may undermine basic needs; comfort, control, self-esteem, wellbeing, belonging, and meaningful existence. The last resort is pain resignation, characterized by helplessness, loneliness, isolation, and alienation. The perception of being a burden on others is also cause for physical symptoms of being fearful of acute repercussions from anxiety and depression. Systematic distortions undermine accurate pain estimation.

Linguistic pain is not to be ruled out. Threats from words and gestures signal adverse reactions to physical, psychological, and social pain. Enhanced activation of neural circuitry occurs both with acute pain and chronic pain. Even thinking or feeling about protracted pain may elicit the same sensations of physical injury itself. Pain-related words and gestures are part of the larger domain of an aversive lexicon. Negatively valence requires more demanding cognitive processing than positively charged information. Unpleasant events, when compared with pleasant ones, evoke more intense emotions, longer sentences, and salient references.

The use of physical pain words and gestures signifies more than a convenient metaphor. Pain references signal valence (positive or negative) arousal, linkage, intensity, word length, and frequency. Verbs convey actions that may cause pain, or indicate antecedents or responses to present centered pain. Not surprisingly, social pain is more easily re-lived (reactivated) than physical pain. Feelings of social pain can be (re)activated or (re) lived long after the painful episode subsides, where feelings of physical pain cannot be easily relived once the painful episode subsides. Affective pain regions are significantly more active when reliving social pain but not more intense when reliving physical pain.

In sum, a tractional model displaces pain or pleasure, comfort, or discomfort, interior or exterior references in favor of wholistic, synthetic, and integrated transfers from one prevailing state or condition to another. Pain is ambiguous. Discomfort rises and falls for all sorts of reasons.

Symptoms are elusive. Distress arises in the midst of other messy stuff, good, bad, and ugly. Painful episodes are difficult to anticipate in advance or after the fact. Pain is necessary, due to stress and strain in daily life. Aversive events function as a warning signal, a cautious need to reconfigure goal-directed aims. Adverse side effects of chronic pain reduce odds of healing or consolation. Constructive means to heal painful episodes are useful mechanisms to restore health, growth, and well-being.

Trauma

Life threatening events are severely traumatic. Post-traumatic stress disorders (PTSD) are intensive, expansive, and boundless. Causalities among military forces rank highest on the list. Mortal risks poste lethal hazards. Killing fields are not a pretty sight. Brutality reigns. Walking wounded pay a terrible price. They bear witness to carnage on a massive scale. Flesh and blood spill all over the place. Land mines detach arms and legs. Explosions penetrate body armor.

Drones shatter small objects. Fear and panic are brushed aside. No way out to escape line of fire. Stress, strain, friction, anger, and rage coincide. After victory or defeat, pack up bags, make sure no dead bodies are left behind. Zip up broken parts in body bags. Smell of decay and death never go away. When causalities multiply, direct exposure to massive carnage must transcend anything that can be said or done in the traumatic aftermath. Old politicians should think twice about sending young persons to travel to foreign lands to fight and die in civil wars of cultural ignorance.

Once veterans return home, domestic maladies will cluster together: wounds, injuries, scars, concussion syndromes, physical liabilities, and diminished estimates of quality of life. Pain, misery, and anguish either congeal or separate, in no causal order. Ratings of PTSD are higher among US combat veterans that what are sustained in the civilian population at large. Lack of control over body, mind, and spirit aggravate lethal symptoms. Flashbacks (re)waken, memory loss, avoidance, distance, numbing, and flat affect combine along with a foreboding sense of shorten future. Other degrading factors include dysphoric arousal, sleep difficulties, nightmares, irritability, lack of concentration, and hypervigilance. Heavy exposure to combat zones leaves fatigued combatants vulnerable to domestic threats of lurking dangers outside their cognitive control. lasting effects: bodily damage, degraded awareness, cranial abnormalities, poor effort, depression and anxiety.

It may take a long time, years, decades to mitigate aftershocks of military combat. Posttraumatic stress disorders (re)emerge later in life as a major mental illness. Lingering distortions are vulnerable to crushing repetition from which escape is difficult or next to impossible to achieve. Brain injuries increase pain severity and decrease recall of detail. Social avoidance and ill health follow a long history of degraded awareness. Guilt, shame, and remorse are ascendant risks: flashbacks, nightmares, self/other blame, negative reactions, and startle response. PTSD qualifies as a major health hazard. Even mild brain injuries can magnify the severity and longevity of post-concussion separation. Lasting complains cluster around reports of pain, fatigue, and memory lapse. Traumatic injury ranks among the leading causes of disability and death worldwide. War related loss during childhood and adolescence are high risk measures of adverse mental health during young adulthood. Suicide ranks among the leading causes of death among U.S. combat veterans who have been exposed to childhood trauma from family problems and abuse before joining the army.

Domestic stress disorders are mental health liabilities. Collateral dame from combat stress disorders are critical factors in low quality of life on the domestic front. The lingering effects of military training can aggravate domestic turbulence by themselves. Insecure family relations produce mixed results, making things better at times, at others making things worse. Multiple traumas can affect major organs, nerve systems, and cardio-vascular damage. Wear and tear from daily stress show even minor daily hassles can have long-term implications for mental health. Daily exposure to negative affect is predictive of distress, depression, and anxiety.

Lifetime exposure to repeated trauma increase risk of bipolar disorder, alcohol dependence, antisocial personality, separation anxiety, and witness to violence. Prolonged intimate partner distress can increase the risk of morbidity, health decline, and low quality of life. Secondary trauma in troubled families are likely, given close proximity of parents and children to daily conflicts. Aggravated distress, disability, and depleted recourses leave fewer capacities to develop more adaptive coping strategies. Misery piles up in small doses to prolong larger impairments in social activity.

Aftershocks can be as painful as traumatic events themselves. Coping mechanisms can be overwhelmed. Flashbacks are revealed in illusions. Negative reactivity may resemble or simulate original causes. Intrusive images provoke hypervigilance. Startle responses interfere with mindfulness, sleep, and relaxation. Irritability is common. Neural circuits aggravate fear, apprehension, or panic attacks. Social activities suffer. People really suffer from traumatic induced depression and anxiety. These diseases are disorders of disconnection. Depression reveals pain, misery, unhappiness, misfortune, and failure. It is a morbid state that remains obscure. The nervous system is shaken and weakened through sadness, fatigue, inhibition, or the inability to take action. Depression intersects with other problems that are difficult to define. Symptoms are diverse. Anxiety is closely aligned. Burdens of ill health can be too much too bear, as indicated by mood changes, hopelessness, or suicidal ideation. Traumatic life events undermine world view, self-esteem, social ties, and lead to hyper arousal and negative alterations in thoughts and feelings.

In sum, conceptual disabilities and emotional liabilities are leading indicators of prolonged trauma.

Unmitigated suffering is widely dispersed along domestic cites of misery and mayhem.

Not even trauma survivors escape unharmed. Impaired social relations tend to interfere with recovery from stress disorders. Resource loss increases risk of major depression and anxiety disorders. Traumatic recidivism is a significant health burden. Prolonged grief, guilt, shame, and remorse also undermine recovery. It is useful, however, for trauma survivors to be able to share fragments of horrible events with family and friends. Disclosure prevents oppressive silence. Social support also helps to mitigate misery and suffering. Broader societal recognitions of victimization are particularly relevant to restorative justice interventions.

Resilience magnifies the capacity to bounce back from loss. Restoration of close relationships helps to compensate for words and gestures that weaken over time. Because trauma is socially mediated, so also is restoration, recovery amenable to congenial and consolatory intervention. Traumatic information can incorporate core principles of safety, trust, collaboration, and encouragement can strengthen affectionate alliances and facilitate post-traumatic growth.

Suffering

It is hard to ignore the question of suffering. No one is immune. Trauma follows catastrophe, fatality, injury, loss. It is possible to live with suffering, in spite of it, not because of it. Mutuality does not afford escape from friction, strife, and pain. Hurt and harm are part of the larger cosmic bargain. Age may be favored over its alternative. There are still lived burdens to bear. Love of life does not dissolve fear of death. Struggle is possible, necessary, but only in a provisional sense.

Human beings are not in total control of what happens but only what they make happen. Survival does not dictate terms but rather follows in line with what permits survival to continue. What it means to be alive, stay awake, and preserve life may still be construed as compensation for what is lost or displaced along the way. Struggle and strain may be favored but only as a course of last resort. If life is virtue, reward, nothing can take its place, not even misery or tribulation without end.

Suffering is necessary, unavoidable, whether tolerable or not. There are limits to what suffering persons can endure, if only to the point where life is no longer worth living (escape clause). Comfort and consolation are not measures of restoration or resolve as a means to make the most out of crushing life-situations. Suffering may not be equally distributed in civic society but everyone is still subject to the same equation. Obsessive preoccupation with individualistic (egocentric) misery may defect attention away from human awareness that everyone must bear witness to unmitigated suffering of everyone else. The universality of human fatality saves us from existential terrors that are not faced alone. Relief comes from shared suffering and collective resolve to do whatever is possible to minimize needless pain and suffering of those who are least able to bear their own burdens alone.

Collective understanding of the misery of others avoids unwillingness to ignore fragments of personal biographies that would otherwise be passed over, disregarded, or ignored. It is possible to be informed by the diversity, disparity, of grim realities, threaten futures, and lost love. Unrelenting distress can magnify gross inequities, injustice, exploitation, and oppression. An intractable problem is how to respond to the anguish of others and to recognize the difference between ordinary suffering and extreme or radical variations at the outer thresholds of life and death.

Terminal conditions can be objects of empathic compassion by those who have not yet reached them. Observation does not equal participation in total suffering but it still registers in mediums of proximity. Willingness to stand by, to be intimately affected, does not eliminate singular experience but total convergence is not possible anyway. There is nothing to prevent longsuffering humans to reach out to each other at the outer limits of life's borders.

Serving as a witness to the dark sides of mortal existence may give way to an ethical and moral compass that gives way to sacrificial interventions. What transforms degraded life forms are prospects of recovery, restoration, and progress, despite risk or cost. Moral detachment is not substitute for dignified engagement in the plight of undignified human beings. Human ability to grasp and comprehend other's suffering can be a critical means to secure social bonds. Knowledge of widespread suffering requires collective struggle against its denial. Integrated alliances can and should be organized to reduce unjustified suffering of citizens as far as possible.

Summary

A worthy life cannot dispense with subversive influence. Strength magnifies matter, energy, vigor, vitality, favorable conditions, affirmative activities, collective knowledge, progressive achievements, and strong bonds. Human impulses must still be reality tested against their complementary opposites. Lived experiences do not unfold in a straight line. Risks must be taken into account: maximize advantages, minimize disadvantages. What matters most is progressive discovery of purpose, meaning, and fulfillment in worthy projects. Prolong life, postpone death. Make the most of what daily life has to offer. Constraints offset opportunities.

Supportive urges add to resilient struggles to what subversive urges take away. Supportive activities promote security. Subversive activities increase insecurity. Mixed motives are not easily separated. Risky decisions are neither clear nor certain. It does not pay to risk people, places, and things for high risk, low reward calculations. The ecological landscape must be preserved for striving subjects to grow, prosper, and thrive in their natural world. Ruthless destruction of earthly surfaces implicates deterioration of life support systems just as well. Safe and secure settlements contribute to creative inquiry. Collective knowledge, emotional intelligence, and empathic regard work together to facilitate the reproduction of viable life forms.

Disruptive habitats magnify health risks. Local communities require life support systems and expansive meaning values. A world of opportunity produces collective engagement in lasting contributions to secular society. An abundant way of life signifies a capacity for growth, expansion, and inquiry. A subversive way of life undermines progressive achievements and unflinching regard for the sanctity of life. All striving subjects are deserving of honor and dignity, unless proven otherwise. Calculated risks give way to make the most of limited opportunities and prevent the worst from taking place. Ruthless destruction of material resources, in contrast, are counteractive to human stewardship. Only illusions from growth models assume that infinite expansion can be sustained on a finite planet.

A strong sense of collective affiliation has artistic, aesthetic value, along with cultural artifacts, icons, and symbols of historic and cultural significance. Social cohesion and cultural solidarity help to preserve support systems; derived benefits include economic prosperity, open exchange of goods and services, and technical innovations. Conversely, subversive influences tend to diminish the density of institutional integrity. Urban blight is a symptom of ruthless exploitation of basic resources. Anarchy and chaos rule where once safe and secure settlements are rendered unsafe and insecure.

Unstable or unsafe neighborhoods, perhaps more than any other single factor, account for why fragile and vulnerable citizens fail to achieve longevity or secure a high quality of life. Disability risks leave nothing in their wake than misery and grief of those who are left behind. Pain registers in brain tissue. Episodic pain and chronic pain overlap and activate similar neural circuitry. Long lasting chronic pain is one of the biggest health problems that deeply impair a troubled person of a productive way of life. Physical, psychological, and social pain intersect, taken together, have a degrading effect on quality of life, well-being, lost attachments, and social adaptation. Protracted pain affects the whole person, body, mind, and spirit.

Linguistic pain is not to be ruled out. Conflated use of words and gestures rive rise to aversive reactions to physical, psychological, and social pain. Pain-related terms are intrinsic features of a subversive lexicon. Misuse and abuse of discourse and dialogue magnify memories of social pain to be (re)activated or (re)lived long after the original pain has dissolved.

Trauma is life threating. Post-traumatic stress disorders (PTSO) are intrusive, intense, and boundless. Mortal risks pose lethal hazards. Military casualties rank highest on the list, followed behind by domestic trauma that follows in their wake. Lack of control over body, mind, and spirit aggravate lethal symptoms; flashbacks, memory loss, numbness, distance, detachment, flat affect, and a foreboding sense of a short future. Dysphoric moods swings, nightmares, sleep difficulties, distraction, and hypervigilance must be added to the list of subversive influences.

Trauma ranks among the leading causes of disability and death worldwide. Domestic stress disorders magnify mental health liabilities. Daily exposure to troubled families is predictive of acute distress, depression, and anxiety. Aftershocks can be as miserable as traumatic memories themselves. People really suffer from disorders of disconnection. Morbid states remain obscure. Traumatic survivors do not escape unharmed. Grief, guilt, same and remorse linger as narrative themes. Hart and harm are part of the subversive lexicon.

Suffering may be necessity, inevitable, unavoidable but there are limits to what disaffected persons can tolerate. Recognition of the universality of human frailty saves struggling subjects from existential terror that need not be faced alone. Relief and restoration require collective resolve to minimize pain and suffering of those who are least able to bear their own burdens by themselves. Cultural alliances can be organized to reduce unjustified misery and mayhem as far as possible.

8

Social Interventions

Human lives are subject to trial and error, gain and loss. Most values are fleeting and transitory; very few are securely put into place. Revision is a way of life. Nothing works well all the time. What first acquires meaning may be rendered meaningless later on. Capacity does not rule out incapacity. Not does compatibility dislodge incompatibility from the scene. Ability may shift into disability. Use does not preclude misuse or abuse. Value and devalue combine. The world passes us by. Life lessons are replaced. Good stuff becomes obsolete. Fame and fortune dissolve in a flash. Wealth is built the same way it disappears.

While there is still time and place, restorative measures have heuristic value. Recovery may be worth the risk. Compensation alleviates distress. Wounds and injuries are not always firmly inscribed. Provisions must be allowed, from illness back to health. Lost love can be reclaimed, imperfectly or incompletely. Repair devices abound. Third party interventions are available from care takers, burden bearers, empathic agents, sympathetic helpers, and health facilities. For every source of trouble or distress, there are multiple sources of humane intervention. What makes life worth living are direct access to resilient forms of renewal and restoration of viable meanings: repair mechanisms, helping behavior, social support, tender mercies, and prosocial benefits.

Repair Mechanisms

Repair aims at reducing distress and restoring tolerance and patience linked with caring and protective response to troubled persons. A realistic account must avoid prejudice or stigma.

It takes effort to transform, invert, reinterpret, or recalibrate both good (desirable) and bad (undesirable) aspects of human encounters. Negative restoration entails the pent-up release of disaffected thought, feeling, and action. Positive restoration involves deliberate effort to forestall, delay, or prevent the perpetration of offensive violations or major transgressions. Repair mechanisms produce strategic efforts to alleviate distress. Restorative efforts come directly into play when social agents are the source of subversive influences. The question of repair tilts back and forth from disputed accounts of who is to blame or the object of blame

Three methods of restorative effort can be identified. The first cluster of cognitive reappraisals places far less emphasis on the search for corrective or remedial strivings and far more on progressive realignment of prevailing standards of social explanation themselves. Implicit repair mechanisms may operate at the fringes or lower thresholds of social cognition. Compensatory exchanges provide allowance for narrative appeal and ploy: excuse, rationalization, self-exoneration, vain appeal to mitigating circumstance, defensive claims of accidental damage denial of bad intent, or special pleading—as temporary impairment. The second cluster of reparative devices places far less emphasis on mutual reactions to clashing standards and far more on the common pursuit of corrective aspects of remedial action. Included are diverse references to spoken confession, modest concession, volitional compensation, face maintenance, reputation building, and reformulated action plans. A spirit of mutual accommodation promotes the discovery of worthy pursuits and common strivings construed as the unencumbered pursuit of high ideals. The third cluster of reflective association is more difficult to clearly specify, presumably due to the sheer density or unspoken cues that give rise to silence that precedes and those that follow, each spoken utterance and each audible sign of contrition, regret, or remorse. Public silence speaks volumes, and the sheer depth of what can be felt in solitude is simply too immense for reliable calculation. The pivotal subject of discursive silence acquires critical importance in the emotional aftermath of social distress. In reflection, contrite persons can decide to mull over what goes wrong and to identify what can be recovered as something that feels fresh or new.

Excuse. Remedial tactics are not often used as a "one at a time" method of resolution; rather they unfold in complex sets, blends, crossovers, and thick composite descriptions that resist precise description. Conceptual quandaries can also give rise to erratic variations and misdirected acts of rationalization and dismissive explanation, whereas blind spots can just as easily lead to distortion, denial, and avoidance of troubles that remain yet undefined, as inexplicable, confusing, or mystifying. A passionate outpouring of clever excuses—often covered with inflated justification, rationalization, or tortured explanation—may be used to reinvent core definitions, realign

215

the scope or scale of prevailing boundaries, or shift direction as a compensatory means of restoring preferred identities or favored modes of social accommodation.

Underneath the surface of explicit denials of harmful intent are subtle indications of tacit strivings and unspoken urges to dilute or diminish the scope or responsibility for unwelcome or adverse outcomes. Personal excuse shifts focus away from actual causes and viable reasons unwelcome news. Causal substitutions, deletions, omissions, and defensive responses are designed to protect the offender's sense of esteem, integrity, or worth. Excuses provide low-risk methods of coping with misguided intentions, faulty performances, disappointing outcomes, and negative implications that may make the respective parties feel better but only after the fact. However, excuses tend to be beneficial when blended with solid explanations rather than self-justification.

As discursive devices, a litany of excuses often imposes an implicit sense of obligation by the offended person to quell, encapsulate, or suppress hostility, resentment, or heated anger toward those who stand directly accused. Personal excuses work well to defer risk of angry outbursts until the offender is given a chance to explain. Excuses that function poorly qualify as unique ploys in which an offensive act is presumed but in which personal responsibility for the misguided act is not. In the manner of a cheap trick, a rapid slight-of-hand, the focus of conflict shifts away from benign intentions of the offender to the disabling influences of other participants. Certain risks of excuse makers occur then they are regarded as deceptive, duplicitous, self-absorbed, or ineffectual, when credibility is low (e.g., when failure to receive corroboration), when goodwill is low (e.g., blame failure on others), and when long-term disengagement occurs (e.g., failed effort to correct deficiency.

Personal excuses cross into unchartered territory when half-heated justifications are assembled as distracting invocations and where offenders may accept some small measure of responsibility for aversive or degraded outcomes. Gestures of pardon and apology also figure in as minor themes based on hints, probes, and forays into multiple efforts to exempt some of the full severity of hash judgments by recasting offensive actions as atypical, unusual, or not a valid view of what the offender may have intended at the time.

Moral control requires offenders to regard themselves as causal agents for harmful outcomes. Therefore, moral excuse may lead to strategic disengagement, which operates through evaluative justification where hurt and harm are reordered as intended for some redemptive purpose; through sanitizing descriptions by way of euphemism and convoluted terminology, such as minimizing or disclaiming; to make a breach of conduct look more acceptable, respectable, or benign; and through exonerating comparisons with more flagrant transgressions. Accused persons are likely, therefore, to reconstruct subversive events in self-enhancing ways consistent with desired images of themselves, even if long-term impressions work to distort recollection of what transpires as a means of justifying their current social status.

Those who stand accused of unfairness or wrongdoing may choose to indulge in dramatic acts of special pleading or excuse making to distance themselves from the stigma or poor performance, unfavorable conditions, or harsh competition. Denials of wrongdoing appeal to unknown or uncertain factors: involuntary causes, conditions, and consequences of mistakes, mishaps, or miscalculations; claims of lack of power to foresee or forestall misfortune; and being forced to do what one would otherwise not say or do, as when one is under pressure, threat, or duress from external powers.

Exoneration requires insight, empathy, and sensitivity toward offenders who inflict needless pain and suffering on others. Justification also requires diminished insistence to hold alleged offenders as solely responsible for their disquieting or disturbing actions. It is not always easy or effortless to acquire a tentative consensus about the magnitude of violations or transgressions in question, much less to offer clear signs of contrition over damage or harm already imposed. Personal accounts of what goes wrong must address embedded matters of fault, failure, blame, and reproach in mitigative tactics aimed at midcourse corrections of downward spirals. Tactics of exoneration may enable offenders to maintain a positive image, minimize larger problems, and avoid retaliation. Persons who are subject to blame and criticism may be inclined to deflect or divert attention away from responsibility by pointing fingers, rationalizing, denying, stonewalling, filling the air with empty words, engaging in ad hominem arguments, and using other means of distorting reality.

What is not clear is how scaled offenses, violations, and transgressions qualify as worthy of remedial compensation. Indirect influences revolve around subtle or vague acts of hinting, humor, hugging, symbolic gestures, tacit overtures, unspoken assurances, tokens, gifts, poetic cards, or flattering remarks. Explicit gestures, in contrast, entrail stronger emphasis on reconstructed modes of verbal dialogue punctuated by acts of pardon, apology, and forgiveness. Instead of one-way transmission or reparative effort, intensive engagement in a difficult and arduous process whereby all affected parties strive to work closely together through difficult, disturbing, or troubling matters and thereby acquire desire and motivation to restore favorable conditions into the foreseeable future. Mitigative tactics also moderate extreme reactive tendencies and cancel out the influence of undesirable traits.

The central decision is whether to risk direct exposure to unknown hazards of direct confrontation or rely instead on passive methods of withdrawal and avoidance. Public notice of wrongdoing or unfairness may well require a great deal of mutual sensitivity and reparative effort to neutralize well-established but highly disruptive feelings, thoughts, and disabling action tendencies. Redefinition of status differences, social disparities, and marked discrepancies may foster acts of acceptance centered on resolve and tolerance of uncomfortable conditions; selective discounting, deflation, or dilution of unfavorable outcomes; or open recognition of better cooperation and discover shared means to repair or restore close bonds. The purpose of emotional mitigation is often to blunt the force or magnitude of mutual antagonism in corrective exchanges designed to restore equilibrium or at least to save face.

Cognitive appraisals of injustice, unfairness, or wrongdoing may entail clever or devious "recalculations" to downsize the scale or scope of offensive allegations in question. Acts if "shaving" and "leveling" occur by faint appeal to mitigating conditions, including unnoticed distress of the offender. Emotional distance from injuries, real or imagined, may be contingent on repeated use of upward comparisons (e. g., far worse things occur to others) or selective indulgence in downward comparisons (e.g., it couldn't have been all that bad). Finally, if the injured party is presumed to have deserved it, had it coming, or merely looking for big trouble, then any alleged suffering can be recast as warranted; hence, empathy toward the guilty party is rendered null and void. Moreover, pursuit of making amends is one useful way to mitigate lingering feelings of guilt or shame. If there is no reason to identify with one's victim, then acts of misuse, abuse, or wrongdoing are, in effect, barely subject to reflective reappraisal. Conversely, a strong desire to make amends can be transformed into all all-inclusive moral imperative or injunction—if anything can be done to restore a sense of fairness or equity in human encounters, it must be done.

Reformulation require reciprocal adjustment and mutual accommodation, whereby troubling exchange relations can be brought into sharp focus, made sense of, and then discussed from convergent viewpoints by a plurality of participants. Reformulated modes of social inquiry may require broad tolerance of cross-checking over prior but faulty exchange that still stand in the way. Since each speaking turn modifies the impact of the preceding speaking turn, shared acts of corrective procedures need not precede willy-nilly but rather stay on course until verbal mentions of trouble, discord, and misery have all received a fair hearing, sufficient at least to vent and air unresolved grievances until a sense of relief is achieved.

Discovery of the means to settling accounts is the price to be paid for admission into the fray. Personal decisions to withholds complaints and irritations are indicative of one's confidence in the ability to achieve opposing goals. Personal acts of reframing facilitate gradual reformation of the interpretive features of faulty or ineffectual aspects of social performance. Personal acts of relational reframing entail active recognition of any salient indications of distance, discomfort, and distress. The ability to reframe problematic conditions opens up the way to diminish the severity of destructive acts and thereby recue estimates of others' responsibility for alleged infractions. Acts of reframing occur each time a victim ceases to be resentful and stops making negative judgments toward a transgressor.

Restorations of damaged human encounters requires considerable abstinence from countervailing forces of vengeance and retribution, both of which thrive on jealousy, refusal to forgive, or reconsider aligned enforcement of punitive verdicts. Likewise, pressing or problematic aspects of difficult may also be subject to selective and strategic recasting, whereby extreme interpretive frames—consisting of excessive features of dualism, absolute thinking, and polarized labels—are revised to appear normal, mundane, or ordinary. Harsh assessments may be diluted, downgraded, or distanced in tacit pockets of explicit agreement and unspoken understanding to deny or else disavow any previously head contentions. Definition slides into redefinition in the manner of calming things down, easing tensions, or making the best of a bad situation.

Subtle speech acts provide a useful alternative to an imperial or demanding style of social injury. Instead of engaging in a dreary litany of harsh directives, commands, or demands imposed on disaffected persons, some assertive, forceful speakers may soften a harsh or abrasive tone by means of indirect appeal to milder inferences and warmer implications. A modest request substitutes from a harsh demand. A subdued warning dampens a rising sense of alarm. Verbal threats based on hints or innuendo minimize the risk of direct confrontation.

Although acts of affirmation and acceptance are enacted explicitly, directly, and quickly, countervailing signs of rejection, disapproval, and disaffection are just as easily deferred, delayed, muted, or mixed with faint praise. Defensive silence thrives on acts of withholding, omitting, or concealing shared recognition of critical, competitive, or contemptuous urges. However volatile acts taken as unforgiven and unforgivable violations of core values may well delay or even prevent and forestall mutual expressions of conciliatory gestures toward the possibilities of constructive transformation.

In the aftermath of intense conflict, offender parties may decide to indulge in stark fantasies of revenge and retaliation interspersed with benign wishes for reparation or conciliation. When close relations are ripped apart from cumulative conflict, antagonism, and animus, any lateral, one-way effort at restoration will be at risk of being dismissed or ignored as incredulous or totally absurd. Misalignments set up in the manner of a stalemate which can be painful to withstand for very long.

To overcome the pain of breach, what matters decisively is shared recognition of unfinished business that stands in the way of progressive effort. Acts of unconditional resolution or restoration require strong resolve to explore issues of offense or violation with shared focus on recovery of mutual loss. The intangible "healing" power from retelling of distressful live narratives includes greater insight into choices and options for added inspiration or greater liberation for what would hold one back

Key measures of close bonds are closely linked to a generous and congenial spirit of accommodation, willingness to sacrifice, and motivation to diminish entangled social ties. Members are likely to adopt long-term outlooks and show uncommon willingness to overlook small-scale aspects of hurt and harm. A strong sense of collaboration promotes greater willingness to engage in beneficial endeavors with relational partners, even at a personal cost.

As motives to avoid direct contact with prior offenders recede, the groundwork is established for diminished resolve to seek revenge or retribution. When congenial partners work together to diminish feelings of insecurity, weakness, and vulnerability, acts of charitable reconstruction are better able to correct severe imbalances in negative sentiments and thereby become subject to redress and reconsideration. Defusing the magnitude of destructive impulses is crucial as preparation for a renewal of shared hope, belief, or faith in better things to come. The case for compensation rests on retelling once sad stories with a renewed happy spin. The credibility of an apology or pardon coincides with the scale or sympathy for the offender.

Acts of reconciliation require a period of healing and recovery so that a tradition of endless quarrels, fights, disputes, and petty bickering can be settled, opposition weakened, acquiescence granted to unpleasantness, and resolution of conflicting views rendered somehow more compatible or consistent. Solid reconciliations take opposing valuations and reform them into something worthy of emulation. A spirit of reconciliation reflects an abiding sense of cohesion and solidarity with kindred spirits.

Mutual efforts to address disturbing questions are confessional in nature, or at least have cathartic form. The day of reckoning for hurt and harm may be formulated around rituals and routines of apology or pardon to validate injured feelings, intuitions, and sensibilities. Spoken apologies often convey a sense a transgressor has felt guilty for suffering. Therefore, part of the emotional cost has been accepted, despite difficulty in owning up to serious violations of mutual sensibility, the victim is less likely to blame or punish in return. Severe trust violations, however, are often difficult to repay, particularly when apologies do not restore misgivings about the offender's sincerely. Refusal to reconcile can be hazardous to one's health and well-being. An unforgiving person may refuse to admit wrongdoing by clinging to cold emotions, hidden resentments, bitterness, even hatred, along with lingering retaliatory urges.

Acts of reconciliation entail valued decisions to forego retribution for hurtful conduct and relinquish claims for restitution. Willingness to forgive facilitates a spirit of recovery, hastens the demise of invisible wounds, and prepares the way for a greater measure of renewal and regeneration. One precondition entails a willingness to subdue anger, rage, or malice, and thereby defect lingering desires to extract reprisal or compensation.

The act of letting go of bitterness and resentment may be brief or prolonged, depending on whether the process of restoration is complete or incomplete and whether all things in question are presumed to be worthy of forgiveness. There are hazards, however, implicit in vain attempts to rescue lose bonds from troubling issues in which nothing is ever settled and virtually everything is left in jeopardy. Passage of time is a strategic aspect of genuine restoration of prior benefits. Intrinsic restoration confers strength, health, healing, and health and renewed commitment to the restoration of intimate relations. Salutary outcomes include uplifting experience combined with renewed desire or sense of obligation not to hurt another person again. Relief affords an added measure of opportunity to regain trust, reconcile, diminish guilt, and achieve closure for distressful events. Invisible wounds recede as offender and offended undertake the difficult task to take the integrity of each party into full account.

Words and gestures do not remove all stains. When everything that can be done, has been done, what remains is the density of silence. Offender parties are left to discovery that even a small measure of silence affords comfort and solace from the harsh effects of careless, abusive, or reckless talk. Exclusive reliance on verbal cues may serve unwittingly to perpetrate severe imbalance in the distribution of sound, sense, and silence.

The security of silence has salutary benefits. One does not have to talk endlessly to repair nonverbal sensitivities. Silence neutralizes the flow of incessant talk into thin slices and minute duration. It takes effort to be silent and stay silent in a noisy world with strong conformity demands for everyone who say something, even if they have nothing to say, except, perhaps, to keep idle chatter going. Quiet withdrawal into the depth of the unspeakable and the unspoken may have redemptive significance. As one ceases to speak, silence is restored.

The restorative value of silence, quietude, stillness, requires tolerance of unspoken comfort. Where there is no longer damage, there is nothing to repair. Intimate comfort enables shared willingness of each party to go for infinitely long periods without saying anything and still not feel awkward at all. Constructive silence helps striving subjects to reconcile differences of opinion without feeling the need to say anything at all. In the final analysis, silence offers sanctuary. Nothing left unexpressed is found wanting, no sense of unfulfillment. Cohesive parties are free to linger just long enough to make each other yearn for things to be exactly as they are.

Tender Mercies

In a rugged society, it is not reasonable to expect repair mechanisms to carry all the weight. Of course, reservations apply to other methods, particularly when subversive influences have a staggering grip on the degraded lives of troubled persons. Damage and danger are far too pervasive to be swept aside. It is, unfortune, however, that appeals to 'tender mercies' are often relegated to subordinate, secondary, or fringe inscriptions of 'soft' or 'meek' techniques of social intervention. Ancient wisdom proclaimed the meek will inherit the earth but in a world of nuclear proliferation that does not seem likely any time soon. Often overlooked is the sheer courage to act in a gentle manner that does not seek to exploit or oppress troubled members of the larger human community.

Mercy shows regard for misfortune.

The first point is that tender mercies are discretionary. Reciprocity is not required. Tenderness does not require public permission. Nor is it necessary to insist that soft qualities are innate, socially constructed, or institutionally sanctioned. It takes only one individual to manifest such admirable qualities. Because these virtues are acts of free will, there is no assurance they will prevail over stronger or malevolent powers. A tender spirit can be given but not taken away. One may refuse to accept tenderness from another but that does not erase the original act from the larger equation. There need be no strings attached.

Tenderness is irreducible and merciful. It is basic. Other good stuff may be construed as correlates: kindness closely followed by sympathy, care, concern, and compassion but what is tender can still stand alone: soft, delicate, sensitive, mild, cautious, affectionate. Aligned values are worthy of sensitive handling. By implication, they are not forcible or rough but rather unable to withstand hardship. Flowers flourish in spring; they do not tolerate blazing summer heat, frost in fall, or cold in winter. Seasonal changes in nature are not mere metaphors for basic human emotions that surge, for a moment, and just as easily fade away, at least without constant cultivation and steady nurturance. Sudden alertness to another's vulnerability may elicit tenderness as a specific empathetic arousal. Tenderness is expressed distinctively. Each instance is protective of the welfare of valued others. Tenderness is to a temporary state what kindness is to a prevailing mood.

Kindness is considerate. It is modest, frugal, desirable. Kindness emerges as more of an effect than a cause of valued benefit. It minimizes comparisons with others. A modest posture of kindness avoids needless distraction. Actions benefit others. Mutual kindness is revealed in the form of loyalty, solidarity, and commitment to a cause greater than oneself. Multiple variations are expansive, from kinship ties, and close friends all the way to strangers in need of assistance. Intrinsic rewarded are more valued than extrinsic benefits. Kindness is verified when it is known and felt keenly.

Small acts of kindness are sensitive to momentary distress and unfulfilled needs. It often occurs at so low a level that it is barely visible. Yet, even small acts of support and help are conducive to larger acts of interventions that prevail over long time spans. In other words, regardless of scope or scale, kind dispositions are not bound by sharp boundaries in time, space, or territory. Kind acts may lack visibility in small increments (speech acts) and still evolve into visible, high level campaigns (volunteers, blood drives, charity services). In a larger sense, a series of kind acts may help to sustain whole lives or whole ways of living well. Kindness encourages deliberate focus on unmet needs that are widened int widened in broader domains of civic activity. There may be no such thing as uniform kindness because it is unstable, unsettled, and shifts up or down, forward or backward, to obtain the greatest benefit to those who have the most kindness to give away without counting risk or cost. Benevolence does not suppress kind emotion but rather supports a surge of sensitive awareness.

Self-directed kindness, care, and concern have a buffering effect on negative life events by lowering defensiveness, blame, and depletion from injury. Detached life styles deplete lived experience of kindness and gratitude. Taken together, they align to promote a wider range of healthful outcomes, including good will that people see in themselves as compassionate and accepting. Kindness and gratitude focus on the present without regard for future implications. Deprivation instills a grim belief that life has treated oneself unjustly. Appreciation for oneself and others are magnified in simple daily pleasures. Appreciation flourishes without set boundaries.

Human generosity is also selective: kinship ties and close relations are favored over others. Intrinsic and extrinsic rewards shift back and forth, usually without balance in what is received or returned. Benefits to others are matters of self-interest, despite the costs. Generosity is meaningful because it is so easily shared. Visibility helps to undermine feelings of anonymity and detachment. Reciprocity is not assured; giving benefits and receiving benefits are not often well aligned in short-term measures of direct reward. Mutual abundance is more likely to lead to long-term payoffs. Short-term generosity implies a gift given without expectation of immediate return, even if the cost to the benefactor exceeds the obligation of return from those who receive the gain. Complex maneuvers (give-and-take) are likely to lead to intangible rewards, namely fortified security, when self-interest and other-interest coincide.

Unpredictable aspects of a generous spirit cannot be denied. Neither can the stabilizing effect of abundant generosity by underestimated as active forces in precarious and insecure alliances with distant acquaintances. In effect, generosity favors proximity; distance inhibits free exchange, particularly when there is not enough to go around (scarcity). General allotments, therefore, are caused less by personal willingness and more by limited supply of what is required to satisfy basic human needs. Proxemic causes of generosity are based on motivated behavior, whereas ultimate explanations favor the adaption of social alliances. The complementary aspects of direct (proxemic) and indirect (distance) allocations must be closely aligned for subversive influences to be undermined.

Generosity flows outward into the external world, without assurance of collective benefits. There is no firm continuity between generous action and cooperative tendencies. Generous acts benefit to the gift-giver, not necessarily to the gift receiver. Perhaps it should be sufficient to recognize a generous person can seek to benefit in all kinds of ways, either from momentary acts or long-term commitments. Multiple motives are implicated, but the one that matters most is the one that is valued by generous persons themselves.

Gratitude returns kindness. Whereas generous acts count as strong emotion, gratitude is calm, quiet. It is a corrective to lack of appreciation. Gratitude is also a counter measure of vengeance.

Even brief episodes may serve to strengthen social bonds and receptive ability to repay benefactors. Gratitude corrects resentment. It also activates sentiments of admiration, respect, and regard for social rituals and congenial routines. Gratitude is receptive to valued benefits. Strong negativity (narcissism) is undermined by positive warmth. Obligations and opportunities congeal together with resilient appreciation. An abiding spirit of thankfulness is welcome. Blessings outnumber burdens. What is acquired means more than what is denied. Gratitude aligned with kindness serves to enhance a sense of connection and satisfaction with daily events.

Gratitude is appreciative of another's presence. Gratitude is a stable response to the receipt of benefits bestowed as a gift, blessing, or favor. An appreciative spirit is easily cultivated and proves efficacious in activating positive emotions. Gratitude is a source of human strength. Grateful persons are often highly satisfied with their lives and they routinely generate positive affections such as happiness, vitality, and hope. In general, grateful persons rank high on prosocial behaviors, empathy, forgiveness, religiosity, and spirituality. Gratitude is manifest as salient, acute, and intense.

Meaningful words and gestures are well endowed with value of the welfare of the benefactor. A grateful mood is more subtle and less easily accessed in conscious awareness that what is afforded by a sudden burst of grateful emotion. Gratitude, spirit, vitality, and inspiration go together as intangible benefits, broad gains, and subtle effects on amicable social outcomes. Strength, virtue, and nurturance enable persons, relations, and communities to thrive and flourish.

Outer limits of gratitude expand beyond the reach of tangible benefits. Affirmation of goodness falls upon oneself, without cause or reason. An abundant sense of gratitude widens with appreciation for life and the joy of being alive. Inspirational feelings do not have to be assigned to social encounters but rather to acute appreciation for the privilege of exploring the beauty of nature. There is cause to give thanks for existence, even if it is not given by anyone or anything. Mortal existence affirms the privilege of 'being' here, for whomever or whatever contributes to life itself. Secular gratitude is manifest in wonder and awe of worldviews, without need to trace back to a myth of origins. A sudden awakening follows from recognition of the material foundations of mortal existence as the ultimate miracle. Astonishment confronts the inability of articulation. Goodness is not self-authored nor self-explained but rather transcends conscious awareness. Ultimate meaning systems do not fall from the sky. They are discovered without appeal to explicit reference or singular authorship. Cosmic gratitude leads to an enlargement of appreciation for what human existence makes possible. What happens to us matters infinitely more than what we make happen. The world makes us possible without the need for us to make the world possible. We are privileged to give thanks for what is given more than what we give back in return.

Humility accepts modesty—human beings do not construe what makes human constructions possible. The joy of being in the world passes all human understanding. Gratitude admits to what is unearned. It has a generative character. Gratitude and generosity congeal together in a shared, exuberant sense of thankfulness for the privilege of mortal existence on a lonely planet. The absence of a supreme benefactor does not preclude gratitude or exclude room for praise without names (of reference). One may give thanks without objects of praise. Inheritance is a gift without gift giver. What can be given away does not require that it is given back.

Repair mechanisms and tender mercies are derived from strong emotions and reasonable applications. Collective impact on subversive influences cannot be calculated in precise form.

Mitigation stands in the way. One, (positive) intentions do not assure (positive) outcomes. Unintended consequences are not easily brushed aside. Two, attractive features of repair and restitution are not always received in a welcome manner. Fear of kindness is not uncommon. Those who refuse to be kind to themselves are unlikely to notice kindness from others. Three, defensive strategies are prone to assign false motives. Lack of worth does not accord with worthy interventions from external benefactors. Three, clusters of multiple cues to relieve distress do not operate in a social vacuum. Four, strength of intervention depends on access to three types of secondary gains: humility, help, and support. Five, fringe aspects of compassion may supplement suppression of subversive influences. Hope, interest, joy, pride, and relief qualify as incidental properties.

Genuine gratitude is a spontaneous response. Humility plays a role because it predicts the ability to receive aid from others and receive gratitude in return. Humility allows recognition that we benefit from others' assistance. Humble persons devote more time to help others, even when social pressures are low. Humility recognizes limits and diminishes Self-preoccupation. It opens the way for more recognition of interests, importance, and worth of others. Appreciation is granted for the abundance of life and the value of all things that contribute to worldly investments. A sense of modesty is not lofty. One is no longer under the illusion of being in the center of anything in any sphere of public life.

Humility is opposed to an exaggerated sense of entitlement or inflated self-importance. It does not comport with an overestimation of one's presence in the greater scheme of things. Cynicism inhibits gratitude. Humility celebrates, capacity, abilities, and gifts, in opposition to defects, deficiencies, and liabilities. Modesty regulates strength of social bonds. A humble person is more likely to be seen as less (inwardly) selfish and more (outwardly) oriented toward trust and commitment to others' welfare.

A generous spirit enables mature adults to invest in vital project designed to create, justify, and validate their place in the wider scheme of things. In a mythical sense, all is well that ends well, despite setbacks, adversity, or misfortune. Over a lifespan, generative adults seek to enable blessings to outweigh burdens, stay sensitive to suffering, and nurture a compelling vision of a sense of life well lived before others. They also seek to produce satisfying endings to life stories, preserve honorable legacies, and sustain faith in the dignity and worth of human existence. Gratitude and generosity combine to promote complex, elaborated, inspiring narratives. Thereby, exchange relations may defeat and keep hope alive. Inspiring themes are available to cope with daily hassles, explain difficult events, and shed light on love, friendship, and creative freedom. A grateful, generous spirit enhances progressive, prosocial values and fortifies interventions to increase and enhance benefit-triggered responses.

Compassion alleviates harsh criticism. Personal acceptance must admit to flaws in self and others without recourse to severe judgments. A kind, gentle sense of self-identity is a precondition for compassion when faced with difficulty. Personal sufferings are shared with other suffering humans. Compassion expands generous tender feelings toward empathy, sympathy, and concern for human welfare. Affirmative value registers as a critical component of common humanity; recognition of suffering, acceptance of universal suffering in lived experience; capacity to be moved by the suffering of others and emotional connection with external distress; tolerance of discomfort aroused by observed distress and motivation to alleviate needless pain and suffering.

The moral component of sympathy for the plight of others' distress registers as a mental faculty for the most basic humanistic impulse. Compassion is costly—when not pleasant to endure. In fact, it may be painful to motive assistance for misfortune. The basic wish is that victims do not have to suffer needlessly and hope for impediments to well-being will be removed. Compassion intensities when suffering persons are subject to adverse conditions over which they could not control.

The ultimate test of helping behavior is whether it reduces unhealthy activity. Helpful intentions do not help where unwanted help prevails. It may take years, decades, to acquire unhealthy life styles. Obsession, compulsion, and addiction are intractable sources of subversive influence. One unit of help matters little to ten units of unhealthy outcomes. Strong alliances must be able to withstand the tug of what pulls them apart. Recidivism is seldom conducive to helpful intervention. Helpful assistance works best when it is prolonged much longer than unhealthy habits that align against it. Bounded limits of helpful and unhelpful assistance are easily crossed. Small increments depend on the preparation of helpers to help and willingness of the helped to receive wanted aid.

Mutual sensibilities contribute to good will and resolute struggle to enhance positive moves and reduce negative setbacks. The more severe the bodily damage, the stronger must be joint obligation to seek amends. Helping behavior matters in direct proportion to the magnitude of observed distress. Thresholds of distress intolerance may lead to reduces levels of helping motives. Useful assistance enables distressed persons to acquire an enhanced sense of independence. Troubled persons are left to struggle with regressive setbacks on their own. Those who are hypersensitive to threatening feedback from attempted helpers may be reluctant to see or accept slight modifications in a positive way.

Helping impulses do not uniformly assist. Unresolved tension, stress, and struggle are real issues, regardless of scope or scale of impediments. Helpful behaviors are arbitrators of mixed outcomes, whether to make things better or to keep them from getting worse. Troublesome matters are not dispensed 'once-and-far all' but rather assemble as collaborative capacity of moment-by-moment progress. Helping behavior is more motivating for those who gain access to prosocial gains and thereby reduce fatigue and frailty.

The capacity for cognitive reappraisal is contingent on the magnitude of risk (threat or sanction) in relation to the magnitude of support (comfort or assurance) available. The open spectrum of possibilities is anchored at one end by a condition of unconditional or unqualified support and at the other end by a condition of total discredit or complete disregard. The opposite of support (credit) is subversion (discredit). When supportive alliances are active, they become a powerful force to sustain and preserve favorable state of affirmation; conversely, when inadequate or defective, they are prone to transform favorable conditions into unfavorable opposition. Supportive conditions include acquired benefits, secure connections, member satisfaction, daily success and intolerance of disruptive influences where close bonds are lacking, ambiguous, or unsettled. Human attachments promote safety, security, working models, empathy, assurance, and congenial responses to personal distress. Unwelcome, unwarranted, or unwanted intrusions align with less generous working viewpoints and low ratings of social satisfaction.

Available social support comes and goes from family, peers, and communal ties, as does attachment to people, places, and things. Support, comfort, and care are related to one's willingness to provide aid to others who are faced with major stresses in daily life. A strong measure of personal support provides warmth and comfort to compensate for deep-seated feelings of disappointment or distress. Firm emotional support is a basic component of the acquisition and maintenance of close ties with significant others.

What matters is how well, or badly, chronic feelings of distressed or disturbed members are acknowledged and elaborated in the course of human encounters. Increased social support and decreased mental distress may be influenced by reduced social distress. Thereby, social interventions can buffer the negative effects of exclusion.

The more striving subjects are heavily invested in each other's lives, the more social support is required to neutralize stress and strain that accumulates over time. Persons who promote social support can often recover from stress, trauma, and burnout better than those who do not. Those who receive social support are less likely to undergo acute distress. Stressful events require reserves of social support to offset the threat of lost resources.

Protective values are increased when personal resources are depleted, deteriorated, or in short supply. Scarce, inadequate, or deficit resources foster greater exposure to tension, stress, and strife which, in turn produce negative affect, vulnerability to mortality risks, depletion of social support, and fewer mechanisms of compensation. In effect, the very persons who need the greatest magnitude of social support are the most likely to acquire the least amount of protective assurance from others. When faced with threats of depleted coping mechanisms, further losses may follow, giving rise to loss spirals and escalating damage. Conversely, generous expectations of available social support are self-perpetuating and, therefore, less sensitive to wide variations in support that actually exists.

Optimal interventions are difficult to achieve, much less imagine, in the absence of social support in the midst of difficult tasks. There is little reason to seek support for routine tasks that can be resolved without stress or strain. More intense levels of social support are required to dislodge subversive influences that cluster over time. Supportive resistance can be a powerful corrective force, when aligned with generous supply of helpful behaviors, to restore prior meaning systems or undermine a distressful state of affairs.

A rich surplus of social support is required to counteract the threat or lost resources. Weak, deficient, or inadequate reserves are vulnerable to negative affect, mortality risk, and poor health outcomes. Oddly, the persons who are need of the greatest amount of assurance are also the least likely to receive an abundance of care and comfort from others. For this reason, social support does not work well in any uniform fashion. It is most urgently needed when it is in short supply. Hence, it is important not to assume that direct access to a generous allotment of social support will prove to be an adequate base for compensation.

Comforting strategies are linked with (a) intimate involvement with distressed others; (b) neutral forms of evaluation; (c) affirmative validation; (d) clear explanations for urgent change; (e) provision for intangible gains—warmth, sympathy, empathy, assurance, for troubled times. Direct visible support can have a negative impact when construed as intrusive; while implicit, invisible support, provided indirectly (not viewed as helpful) can circumvent negative implications. The ultimate test is not which type of helping behavior blocks out subversive influences but rather whether it serves as a useful mechanism to heal old wounds.

Prosocial Influences

Repair mechanism and tender mercies contribute greatly to social interventions. Subversive influences, however, are powerful forces. Progressive activity does not reverse or neutralize hurt and harm in a uniform way. The transitory and fleeting appeal of strong emotion is a necessary but insufficient means to undermined, reverse, or correct harmful outcomes. Prosocial influences are widely available to protest, reverse, or correct sharp imbalance in active social systems. It takes a great deal of strength to protect, nurture, and benefit others.

Not everyone possesses the social skill to provide aid to others' distress. Persons who are weak or defective in exchange relations are unlikely to have direct access to a surplus of energy and vitality needed to correct injustice. Flagrant focus on self-interest is also an impediment which is more likely to make things worse than to make them better. Improved levels of health and welfare are laudable goals but not always feasible or plausible. Collective knowledge is required to know how to galvanize prosocial influences to make a decisive difference in human welfare.

What stands out are benevolent ways that individuals use to support, help, and assist others in times of need. Personal responsibility and social accountability encourage striving subjects to maintain positive identities and fulfill collective purposes. Feelings of sympathy, empathy, and sensitivity to the plight of others may activate altruistic motives to improve the welfare of struggling persons. Social systems strengthen attachment bonds with attendant virtues of loyalty to lofty causes. Explicit contact promotes cooperation, reduces pluralistic ignorance, and coordinates participation, and facilitates the preservation of close bonds. Conversely, social isolation or exclusion has the opposite effect of reducing willingness to help, assist, volunteer, or cooperate in shared benefits. Also striking is the desire of prosocial persons to maximize their own and others' outcomes. Prosocial orientations accentuate affective quality, interactive frequency, and social stability. Preference is given to the equity rule out of fairness concerns as opposed to efficiency aspirations. Under favorable conditions, prosocial behavior distracts attention from troubles, enhances meaning, value, purpose, improves daily moods, and facilitates progressive socialization. What qualifies as a prosocial influence is, in fact, an open pathway of effective daily functions, actualized potential, and life satisfaction. Moral judgments must reconcile conflicts in which personal needs or desires clash with felt obligations toward others.

When judged by a sufficiency standard, fully functioning person are able to function fully with each other much of the time. There is intrinsic pleasure in keeping good company. Happiness and meaning mingle freely, Comfort abounds. Shared efforts work through issues large and small. Striving subjects acquire valued subject matter to form a unified, cohesive bond. Intense exchanges exert a centric force, an expansive momentum, a life force that binds kindred spirits closer together.

Optimal states, living fully and fully functioning, are shared with healthy persons who minimize risk, threat, and adversity by maximizing safe, secure, and stable conditions for future encounters to take place. Affectionate, adaptive, and attentive working alliances promote thin defenses, open styles, and shared resistance to whatever can go wrong or slide downhill. Unspoken acts of help and care are sources of healing and renewal. Words or gestures expressed harshly, carelessly, or recklessly must be kept in check. Multiple expressions positive emotions—love, care, joy, happiness, interest excitement—provide an invisible buffer against regressive expressions of anger, fear, and sadness.

Prosocial influences acquire strength from intrinsic motivation, perspective taking, empathy, efficacy, resilience, and commitment. Intrinsic motivations are less strategic, calculated or manipulative. Victims of distress acquire aid from alert observers who are determined not to abandon or betray but rather remain steadfast in loyalty to sympathetic alliances. Intrinsic motives blend well with emphasis on being fully present for others in times of urgency. Intrinsic motivations comport with emphasis on helping others and gaining feedback that signifies competence. Intrinsic aspirations relate to feelings of self-acceptance, affiliation, strong alliances, and physical health. Complex urges entail selective engagement in social interventions for no apparent cause, rhyme, or reason other than what a benevolent person seeks to fulfill.

Rewards and costs are reality tested as events that strengthen resolve and weaken further effort to achieve some distant end. Acute tensions may prove to be a mixed blessing. Intrinsic motives produce more immediate need satisfaction than extrinsic striving. Prosocial encounters favor shared outcomes that provide their own reward. Release of words and gestures can be a source of satisfaction right on the spot. Shared gratifications are directly available and commonly available rather than delayed when only extrinsic gains are at stake. Intrinsic motivations are fulfilling rather than depleting, uplifting rather than downgrading, and honorific in the best sense of the term.

Perspective taking is valuable. It pays to view suffering from multiple vantage points. Flexible observations are spontaneous, creative, and innovative. Inflexible references, in contrast, are impulsive and reactive. Multiple perspectives are designed to share benefits in a fulfilling, rewarding, and satisfying manner. Flexible acts of perspective taking are aligned with proactive expressions and responsive styles that are competent on a personal level and compatible on a relational level. Flexible exchanges promote state of synchrony and stay closely aligned over extensive timeframes. What emerges is an implicit notion of what others may feel, think, say, or do. Much depends on the larger ability to separate an observer's direct experience before others from one's indirect sense of what others may experience from an alternative viewpoint. It is a critical yet risky enterprise to be sure. One cannot merge with others without being able to separate from others too. Boundaries of self and other are not always easily defined with confidence or accuracy.

Effective perspective taking requires a (decentered) displacement of a first-person view to greater proximity to the unfolding perspective of others. Swift adjustments from first (I), second (You) and third (US) personal viewpoints are critical (without getting struck in self, other, or mutual contrasts). Prosocial encounters regulate and reinforce multiple-perspective-taking capacities, abilities, and skills. There is no need to posit strict reciprocity in member's willingness to shift rapidly among first-person, second-person, and third-person positions in the larger system. Empathetic perspective taking and emotional intelligence both qualify as adaptive mechanisms in amicable exchange relations.

There may be strong striving to acquire insight, creativity, and illumination of others' status, and take their welfare, vested interest, or cultural bias into account. Convergence of contrasting perspectives displace one-sided, slanted, negative views. A rich combination of specific and general views is allowed to expand, flourish, and multiply, Instead of insisting that one privileged definition prevails, multiple perspective taking allows for common recognition that the definition of a social system is all of the respective definitions added up to form a unified sense of what transpires along the way.

Empathy predicts generous responses to distressed others. Empathic sentiments are more easily aroused in cases of people, places, and things for which one cares deeply. It is absent from situations of indifference, distance, or detachment. Empathic agents are able to show care and concern for the troubles of others, particularly in adverse situations in which people suffer greatly. However, empathic pain can be intolerable, when it "rubs off" on the plight of victims and observers alike. Empathy is a scarce resource. It is often needed most when it is in short supply. Because it is so difficult to acquire, it cannot be taught in self-help books or glowing internet claims. It is subject to ruin, ignorance, or disregard. Therefore, the scale and scope of empathy varies greatly from one trouble encounter to another. Distressed distinctions between suffering persons can be blurred by abstract (aloof) thinking and emotional distance.

Deep empathy is different than surface recognition. Genuine sympathy promotes greater appreciation for what takes place (in the present tense) and for accepting others for who and what they say and do. Allowances recognize nullities—weaknesses, shortcomings, liabilities. One-way empathy does not preclude two-way exchange, although there is no guarantee either way. Strong attachments and sensitive responses to the troubles of suffering persons are likely to activate assurance. Empathetic exchanges promote free associations that work well to bring people closer together without driving them apart.

Human empathy, whatever the driving force, depends on how much, and in what way, one person values another's welfare, independent of selfish interest, hidden agenda, or duplicitous motives. Empathetic activation increases, therefore, in direct relation to the magnitude of others' unmet needs. The main motive is to relieve distress. This ideal is complicate by risk. It is one thing to identify with what makes others happy or sad. When empathy slides into sympathy, there may be no gain in social support or helping behavior. In fact, intense sympathy may lead back to greater observed distress, construed as aversive reactions of apprehension, discomfort, or anxiety. Excessive empathy may hinder more than help to minimize distress. Another precaution. In a divisive, hostile, or vengeful climate, any sign of a desire for relief may be resented (might makes right, meekness signals weakness). Oddly, empathy exists as a threat, an object of ridicule, where rough and tumble may triumph over soft and proud. Defects in empathy are likely to diminish tenderness and compassion in social conflicts, enforce rigid perspective taking, and interfere with distress of offended victims.

Efficacy. It is easy to feel comfort when things are going one's way. In troubled times, however, a strong sense of efficacy may be in short supply. Personal efficacy is defined as global confidence in one's ability to perform difficult tasks. Benefits accrue from mindful awareness: strong striving, explicit intention, strategic planning, forethought, impulse control, unspoken reflection, and cherished pursuits. It can be enacted by proactive initiatives, by proxy that relies on others to act upon one's behave, or shared endeavors to fulfill multiple goals.

Personal efficacy is not a matter of what people possess, but rather what they profess to be able to achieve. Efficacy predicts future activity while controlling for prior failures. What registers as success may serve to strengthen efficacy beliefs, whereas what qualifies as failure may weaken resolve to confront a disabling outcome. Equally striking, personal efficacy protects against relapse into unfavorable habits, but also strengthens desire to pursue favorable options.

Efficacy judgments vary greatly: (a) level of difficulty, (b) strength of persistence, despite obstacles, and (c) competence across a broad array of rigorous tests. Personal efficacy shapes selected course of action directly, and indirectly shapes motivation, affect, and goal-directed aims. Personal conviction may also influence productive thinking or minimize pessimistic reactions in the face of adversity. Self-efficacy promotes positive views, prosocial values, and diminished inclination to engage in moral sanctions for harmful conduct. Thereby, it counteracts rumination or nationalized urges of vengeful retaliation. Stable abilities and skills work together as a useful framework that explains and predicts future success.

Persons with strong efficacy beliefs, when faced with difficulties, will try harder, whereas those who doubt their own abilities and skills will quickly give up. What matters is a good fit between personal strivings and collective efficacy values. Efficacious persons engage in quicker recovery from setbacks. Level, strength, and spread of efficacy beliefs are linked to successful outcomes, pursuit of critical goals, reliance on demanding standards, and willingness to explore novel options. Personal efficacy is protective. Feelings of strength, resilience. Confidence, and self-regard predict decreased levels of neurotic symptoms.

Generalized efficacy serves as a vital defensive mechanism by reducing intense conflicts. Weakened impulses of criticism protect issues of separation, autonomy, control, and self-worth. Personal efficacy integrates reason, analytical thinking, goal planning, faith in potentials, and resolve to obtain goal-directed aims. Efficacious activities influence physiology, especially the immune system. Strong emotion, affect, and mood encourage healthy practices with ability to confront serious health issues.

Resilience promotes ability to recover from negative events through effective use of positive coping responses with precision and specificity. The protective power of resilient response is also a useful antidote to stress, threat, depression, and ill health. Resilient persons use protective devices to maintain a semblance of equilibrium when confronted with critical issues. The more resilient persons are able to construe traumatic events in an integrated, coherent manner, the more likely they will recognize benefits from critical situations as a way to gain insight into tragedy and learn about themselves, others' anguish, and the world around them.

Multiple, unexpected pathways lead to resilient recovery. Lack of resilient response is often indicative of such adverse factors as lack of social support, low intelligence, poor education, family instability, prior psychiatric history, and dissociative disorders. Conversely, relative absence of such adverse factors is predictive of more rapid recovery from extreme distress. Moreover, resilient persons are likely to benefit from a healthy profile prior to major loss, exhibit hardiness that stems from renewed dedication to find meaningful purposes in life, plus strong belief that one can adapt, cope, learn, and grow from a mix of positive and negative outcomes.

Resilient persons appraise traumatic events as less threatening, rely on inner strength and confidence, and use active coping skills and social support to deal with inevitable distress. Resilient persons generate constructive and uplifting emotions, thoughts, and feelings to bounce back from adverse stress. Acquired resources include self-enhancing devices, repressive coping skills, humor, and wellness-promoting beliefs. A resilient spirit shows how to obtain good outcomes, despite setbacks, resistance, obstacles, or threats to social development. Individual resilience and hardiness go together.

Hardiness take into account inherited vulnerabilities, weaknesses, and shortcomings. Constraining forces and limited factors are set in motion in relation to resilient beliefs about control, challenge, decisive action, perspective taking, assistance, regard and encouragement, Without hardiness, one may take the course of least resistance, depend on worn out rituals, and stagnate the quest for meaning, purpose, and satisfaction over the life course. Resilience, hardiness, and courage work together to tolerate risk, accept challenge, opportunity, and achievement, despite uncertain or unknown obstacles that stand in the way.

Resilience encourages discovery of a sense of fulfillment that is enhanced by the process of reality testing, learning, and reframing from living through the effects of one's cherished choices and decisions in daily life. Personal resilience is a potential form of preventive medicine to diminish the risk of compromised achievements, suboptimal outs, and reduced expectations for the future. Resilient persons exemplify character strength, promote models of human flourishing, and engagement I virtuous activities for their own sake. Humanistic virtues coincide: appreciation of beauty, creativity, curiosity, fairness, gratitude, hope, integrity, love of learning, modesty, humility, persistence, prudence, and zest.

Personal commitment is also directed at the welfare of others. Strength of concern is measured in terms of persistence, accommodation, and willingness to sacrifice. Attractive strivings overcome repelling factors. Enduring attachments entail feelings of loyalty, devotion, obligation, and salient bonds. Willingness to share positive sentiments maybe enhanced by willingness to shared negative feelings toward outsiders, rivals, or third parties. Willingness to express strong emotion occurs under conditions of high communal strength than under low communal strength.

Positive expressions of joy, respect, and admiration induce feelings of admiration and gratitude. Strong commitments predict benign appraisals of violations or transgressions in compensatory ways that strengthen reasons for staying in a bonded relation.

Strong commitments are enacted in routine fashion: showing support, respect, working together, and repeating vows. Reciprocal commitments afford protection from subversive or destructive responses. Strength of commitment provides an implicit obligation to keep one's vows, remain loyal and accessible in times of need. Investment emphasizes labor-intensive effort to stay heavily engaged. The ties that bind may also unwind. Fluid rather than static properties must be subject to stress, challenge, or disruptive change.

Relational commitments depend on reciprocal adjustment and mutual willingness to sacrifice for a larger cause, which provides multiple tests of members' prosocial motivation. Commitments are likely to increase when satisfaction is high, when outside options or alternatives are poor, and when mutual investments are very strong. Secondary benefits include strong urges to forgive and forget minor complaints together with equal resolve to restore health and well-being on a regular basis. Commitment is also linked to resilience construed as shared willingness to deal with what does not work out well. Thus, mutual commitment provides both a reason and a justification for telling the truth, even when it is difficult to own up to less than desirable motives, intentions, or outcomes. An added bonus is shared ability to talk about the resilient meanings as a productive mean to preserve intimacy.

Summary

Social interventions are a critical means to nurture human existence. Multiple meanings of a life well lived are never settled or secured. There is no absolute reality, only the ones that are reality tested in an open expanse of creative inquiry. There is tension, therefore, between worthy experience and unworthy substitutes. Resolute claims to what can make a life worth living must be reality tested against the frictions of the daily grind.

Human beings are finite creatures who do not have access to what keeps anyone alive, alert, and fully invested in ultimate concerns. Questions of dignity and worth are not (self-evident) presumptions but rather proven in resilient and viable resolve to stay the course and stand the test of time. Mortal existence unfolds as a promise, without insurance, master plan, or timeless truth to guide the way into an unpredictable and precarious future. There is only one life to live, to make the most of what is accessible, with no second chances, no short cuts, no secrets, no way to start out all over again. Eternal security eludes human grasp.

Social interventions are necessary. Daily existence is subject to trial and tribulation, trial and error, gain and loss. Coveted aspirations are fleeting and transitory. No strategy or tactic may be expected to work well all the time or in all places. Capacity, ability, and skill are subject to use, abuse, and misuse. Restorative efforts have heuristic value. A life worth living requires compensation for what is lost or displaced along the way. The grim reality of everyday life is the ultimate standard by which distinction between right and wrong, good and bad, truth and lie, are ultimately judged. Repair mechanisms would not be necessary if there was nothing to repair. Hurt and harm are unavoidable, along with wounds and injuries, without access to means of recovery or restoration of once favored conditions. Without methods of compensation, there would be nothing left but to sink into a downward spiral of hopeless despair. It takes effort to test the difference between good and bad, right and wrong, to better know the difference and act accordingly.

Corrective strivings are designed to reduce subversive influences to tolerable levels of forbearance. Compensative exchanges favor realignment of misguided or misdirected goal-directed aims. Adaptive change favors moderation, temperance, and relief from extreme pressures or radical viewpoints. Silent reflection takes the place of excessive reliance on verbal cures. Rationalization appeals to excuses for wrongdoing. Evocative claims shift attention away for real issues in search for distractive and deflective substitutes. Lamb excuses are low-risk devices to cope with high-risk faults and failures. They are also useful ways to minimize personal participation in collective mistakes. Deception and duplicity are cheap tricks but ineffective ways to correct for regressive setbacks. Flagrant denials of wrongdoing are likely to multiple insofar as they remain undetected or covered up in abstract or obscure vocabularies.

Exoneration requires insight and sensitivity to wrongdoing. Denial of responsibility appeals to lack of power to prevent misfortune. Justification diminishes insistence to hold alleged offenders as solely responsible for disturbing actions. Tactics enable offenders to maintain positive identities, save face, minimize harsh judgment, and avoid retaliation. Those who are subject to blame or criticism may deflect attention, by pointing fingers, rationalizing, denying, stonewalling, or using other distortions to avoid reality. Emotional mitigation is designed to blunt the force of antagonism as tentative ways to restore equilibrium. The act of making amends is a useful way to dilute feelings of guilt or shame.

Reformation regulates and adjusts attention so troubled matters can be brought into sharp focus. Reconstructed activity must tolerate revision of prior but faulty exchanges that stand in the way of progressive realignments. Shared means to settle accounts is the price to be paid for collective accountability. Reframed viewpoints entail active recognition of faulty or ineffective activity and pave the way for better estimates of alleged infractions. Restoration of damage requires abstinence from vengeance and retribution. Mutual redefinition calms things down, eases tensions, and makes the best of a bad situation.

Acts of reconciliation give way to a period of reflection. Endless quarrels, disputes, fights, and petty bickering can be settled. Subconscious reconciliation takes opposing valuations and reframes them into something worthy of emulation. Willingness to address troubling issues are confessions in tone and texture, or at least cathartic features. Shared recognition of hurt and harm can be reformulated around rituals and routines of apology and pardon to validate injured sensibilities. Effective reconciliation entails valued decision to forego retribution and relinquish claims for restitution. Forgiveness facilitates recovery.

Willingness to subdue anger, rage, or malice may deflect lingering desires to extract reprisals. Silence neutralizes the flow of words and gestures. A period of silence, quietude, stillness, enables greater tolerance of unspoken comfort. Tender mercies show regard for misfortune. They are discretionary. Acts of volition do not assure they will prevail over malevolent powers. Nonetheless, a gentile spirit can be freely given but not taken away. Tenderness is singular, irreducible, and merciful. Kindness is also considerate, modest, fragile. It minimizes social comparisons and avoids needless distraction. Abundant kindness is revealed in a quest for a cause greater than self-interest.

Kindness, care, concern, and gratitude have a buffering effect on negative life events. They align with healthy motives, good will, and compassion. Generosity is selective. It flows outward, from kinship ties and close relatives over distant acquaintance. Generosity favors proximity; distance inhabits exchange, particularly when there is not enough to go around (scarcity). Gratitude returns kindness, corrects resentment, strengthens social bonds, and repays thankfulness. Abundant gratitude widens with appreciation for life and the joy of being alive.

Humility accepts modesty. Gratitude, generosity, and humility congeal together in an exuberant sense of thankfulness for the privilege of shared life on a lonely planet. Repair mechanisms and tender mercies align against corrosive effects of subversive influences. Compassion matters. The basic wish is that victims will not suffer needlessly. Helping behavior is designed to reduce unhealthy habits. Social support magnifies opportunity to transform unfavorable conditions into favorable alternatives.

Strong attachments promote safety and security. Comforting strategies encourage intimate involvement with distressed others. The ultimate test of repair mechanisms and tender mercies is whether they combine to heal old wounds.

Repair mechanisms, tender mercies, and prosocial influences contribute to the strength and resilience of social interventions. All three clusters are designed to benefit others. Subversive factors, however, are not easily dispatched, even under favorable conditions. Harmful outcomes are difficult to correct. Prosocial activities are widely available in the social fabric, as a means to protest mindless perpetuation of social inequities. Collective responsibility is aligned to alleviate the plight of suffering persons. Optimal conditions enable striving subjects to function fully with other fully functioning persons most of the time.

Prosocial influences activate intrinsic motivation, multiple perspective taking, empathy, efficacy, resilience, and commitment to a worthy cause. Victims of distress acquire aid from alert observers who are sympathetic to their cause. Human suffering may be construed from multiple vantage points in dynamic social systems. Efficacy favors empathic regard, confidence in the ability to perform difficult tasks, facilitate recovery from subversive events, and shared preservation of close bonds. Social interventions are creative ways to make mortal existence worthy of honor and dignity for all members of the larger human community.

www.ingramcontent.com/pod-product-compliance
Lightning Source LLC
Chambersburg PA
CBHW050224270326
41914CB00003BA/553